Jenny Ha
Association of Sexual
and Relationship Therapists

Think
SEX

JENNY HARE

vega

A catalogue record for this book is available
from the British Library.

ISBN 1-84333-010-5
Printed by CPD Wales, Ebbw Vale

© Vega 2001

A member of the Chrysalis Group plc

First published in 2001 by
Vega
8-10 Blenheim Court
Brewery Road
London N7 9NY

Visit our Website at www.chrysalisbooks.co.uk

Contents

Introduction

A New World of Sexuality –
Free and Irrepressibly Joyous

We're poised at the brink of a new sexual age. This is the beginning, the building, of something amazing. We have the opportunity to give our sexuality its full potential, confidently living and harmonizing with its energy and joy.

The foundations are strong. For the first time in the modern Western world, men and women are free to enjoy their sexuality, whatever their orientation, to the full. The equality battled for by the suffragettes and the freedom from unwelcome pregnancy enabled by effective contraception brought us closer to this point in the last century. But it would take far longer than we realized to adjust to the new sexual and social climate and to work out safe-sex strategy. The 1990s still saw us struggling to make sense of the new freedom. Underlying the growing abundance of information on sexual and relationship technique was a mood of frustration and confusion. Sex rarely lived up to best expectations, and relationships continued to crash or fizzle disappointingly.

There was an omission. Glaring. Huge.

We'd missed the essential truth

Fulfilling sexuality and mind-blowing sex aren't dependent on skilled sexual and relationship technique. Best sex is all about you – your feelings, your attitude, your zest for life. Your self-esteem. Your mind and spirit as well as your body. It's about the completeness of sex within the wholeness of your life. And it's about recognizing the truth that sex is essentially good – a dynamic force energizing you individually and in relationships. There is far more to it than a physical high or a fertility passage – your sexuality is at the heart of your being and has an impact on everything you are, everything you do.

> *Harness the potential joy – it's up to you.*
> The most inspiring part is that it's up to you – you hold the keys. Great sex is a life-transforming poem of mind and body. Thought is always the leader and thought is yours. With your mind you can use your sexuality not only to improve your life, but to generate energy and vibrancy in the world around you.

Great sex happens when thought, feeling and sensation impact

When your mind, your senses and your emotions come together as you're having sex the alchemy is amazing. The highest charge of physical pleasure fuses with spiritual and emotional joy. It's the sex of dreams. The most perfect satisfaction. The deepest fulfilment.

And it doesn't have to be a rarely discovered, tantalizing treasure. Confident fulfilling sexuality and mind-blowing sex can be yours.

▶ ***The key is to bring your mind into the equation.***
It's the elixir of sex, the fount of joy.

Good sex isn't exclusive to the chemical high of being 'in-love'. It isn't dependent on excitement or complicated techniques or exotic ideas and rituals. Tantric sex, the *Kama Sutra* and other ancient sexual arts have much to offer and can complement great sex, but they aren't essential for sexual bliss. Great sex isn't purely about freedom either – people tried that in the sixties and soon found it wasn't the key to great sex. Great sex isn't scary or difficult or seedy, ever. And it needn't be elusive or temporary.

▶ ***Great sex is all about thought. Your thought –
your mind.*** Sex isn't just a physical phenomenon – you need to think sex.

The mind not only controls all your erogenous zones – it is the most erogenous zone of all. Every aspect, every nuance of sexual pleasure is processed by your mind and you can lead the way with thought too.

Beautiful, mind-blowing sex is for you – your gift. And once you know how to encourage it into your life it will flow naturally and you'll wonder whatever stopped you from enjoying it before.

The mind and body connection is the essence of real sex – the sort we yearn for, body and soul. The in-love link is too elusive, too ephemeral to wait for or rely on. But you yourself can encourage, welcome and nurture your sexuality now and throughout your life. You can use your mind to appreciate and link the gifts of your senses. You can use your mind to free your emotions to express your true feelings. And you can say YES! to a full understanding and appreciation of your sexuality and sexual wishes.

It depends on who you are and what you really want

An erotic, sensual, satisfying and mindfully sizzling sexuality shimmers with promise, waiting for you, whatever your age and gender and whether you are heterosexual, bisexual or gay. You can choose what you want – in life, from sex, from your partner or from solitude. Single or in a relationship, your sexuality can have a hugely positive influence on your well-being as a source of pleasure, an enhancer of self-confidence, a fundamental sense of self-knowledge.

Alone or in a relationship, take charge of yourself. Do what is right for you. You hold the keys to your own sex life, sexuality and sensuality. You have a deep power to enjoy the sublimest of pleasure, satisfaction and internal joy.

It's a journey of enlightenment, inspiration and joy. Not to mention pleasure, fulfilment, and contentment. And you are led along by your seven senses, translated by your mind, every stage of the way, into a beautiful sexual script.

Seven senses? Yes seven. They are the secrets of confident, joyous sexuality. And, if you want, mind-blowing sex. But – always – your mind leads the way …

Enjoy!

Part 1

Sex Starts *with a Thought*

♥ ♥

Good sex – best sex – starts in the mind

Every aspect of the whole, complex, glorious gift of sexual pleasure is down to your thoughts. Even the feelings, urges and passions? Yes, you are at the controls and can steer and pace your emotions. If it's your wish, you can give free rein to joy, where mind, body and spirit unite in sublimely complete sensation. In the acceptance and appreciation of your sexuality your mind is the leader.

Your sexuality is not at the mercy of fortune. Single or in a relationship it's yours to enjoy to the full – an intrinsic part of your whole being. So whatever your gender or sexual orientation, welcome, care for and take pleasure in your sexuality. Make your attitude, along with the external and internal conditioning that create it, positive. It's not just possible, it's a feel-great process.

The Miracle Of Sex

Sex begins as a thought ...

Whether prompted by an external erotic trigger or an internal hormonal impulse produced by the endocrine system, it's the accompanying thought that leads you on. Sexual feelings rely on the ongoing co-operation of your mind to progress into desire and arousal. Whether the turn-on curves upwards steadily or escalates fast, the way to high sexual excitement and into orgasm is fired, all the way, by the brain.

The minute recognition of your sexuality crosses your mind (and that happens every few minutes for most men and women) the brain's centres – the limbic system, hypothalamus and cerebrum – leap into action. The limbic zone gives the go-ahead to sexual behaviour, pleasure and feelings. It also has a protective side, always alert to the need for caution. Listened to, and kept in sensible perspective, it's a good friend. The limbic system also controls an olfactory centre, responding to others' pheromones and triggering your own.

The hypothalamus responds directly to genital stimulation and has a lot to do with sexual arousal and orgasm. It's the chief organizer of your sexual reflexes and hormonal output too. Meanwhile, the cerebrum enables you to think sex and file sexual experience, past and present. It's the astonishingly sophisticated overall sexual control centre and it responds to your direct wishes and commands.

And your mind leads you on ...

Although it may sometimes seem as though your sex drive has a mind of its own, you are the driving force – enabling, guiding and fuelling it. Your response to sensual stimulation inhibits or facilitates turn-on. And your thought processes constantly modify sexual reactions and reflexes too.

> *All the multiple sexual influences to which you're responding at every moment are under the overall control of the higher centres of your brain.* That's YOU. Your power, your energy, your exciting, irrepressible sexual potential.

Decide you're not sexually willing, consciously or subconsciously, and the sexual pathway is blocked. Whether alone or with a friend, if you go ahead unwillingly your sexual responses will be a non-event in the arousal and satisfaction stakes, however good the technique.

But if the answer's yes, you do want sex, you'll respond with further erotic stimulation. This could be pure thought – even without direct sensual input, your

Thought ~ awareness ~ shall I/shan't I? ~ yes ~ thought ~ action ~ thought

mind will fire the train of physiological links via an ultra-sensitive neurological network.

You Have to Feel Good About It

The capacity for sexual pleasure is your personal gift and if you value it and want to get the best from it – with brilliant sex and fulfilling sexuality – only say yes when you know it's right for you. The timing, your partner, your personal sense of integrity and your protection all need to be right and you'll know, if you listen to your logic and your heart, when they are.

Thought, Go-Ahead, Action

The instant the thought is there your brain is on standby alert. With your express permission – and hopefully an enthusiastic YES for full power – it activates your nervous system, down-loading a complex cocktail of cellular and hormonal activity. Sexual 'messengers' skate down the spinal cord energizing your response through an amazingly intricate physiological system involving just about every part of your body. Your erogenous zones are primed and, sometimes instantaneously, sometimes shortly afterwards, there'll be a genital reaction too.

At every stage of the way, upfront or subliminal negative thinking can smash a link. If it does it can scupper the whole chain reaction. But given your continuing enthusiasm, or a swift gathering together of positivity for a fresh charge of energy, the sexual responses will forge on, circling back to the control centres of the brain, for as many times as it takes to reach the point of no return before short-circuiting and tripping the system into an explosion of feeling. Climax!

Your brain primes every moment, every atom of your response. You switch on the system with a thought and your input keeps it alive. Your allies are awareness to the effect it's having on you, willingness to enjoy and eagerness to keep participating – all increase the sensations and help energize the process.

Sex involves mind and body. But the body is mind-led and each link of the sexual circle through desire, arousal and satisfaction depends on *your* thinking, *your* mind. You tell your body yes or no to sexual pleasure.

You may already know how it is when you switch off the action? You're having sex with someone willingly and enthusiastically, then for no reason a disassociated thought crosses your mind – you've forgotten something important, maybe, or something about your partner is a turn-off. Either way, your arousal plummets. The instant you were distracted you lost contact with the express wish to be enjoying the sex and the system shut down. That's how powerful your mind's attention is.

Hot hormones?

The sex hormones have a big effect on the sexual circle of drive, desire and response, but they're only produced in enough quantity to tip the balance into desire and arousal and on into satisfaction. Testosterone is most associated with men's sex drive, oestrogen and progesterone with women's along with smaller amounts of testosterone. But they can't alone create sexiness or fulfilment – you think it into being. And, without your initial and continuing motivation, hormones alone can't build your sexual response either – they just enable it.

Women are especially sensitive to monthly hormone balance changes, but much can be done to ease these highs and lows. The seven secrets smooth the path, so keep reading for inspiration. As a start to encourage a comfortable hormone balance follow this basic plan:

✻ ✻

RECIPE FOR A HEALTHY HORMONE LIFESTYLE

Think of hormones as your sexual friends, not enemies – they keep you in good shape, physically and mentally, but you need to take care of them too. Your way of life has a tremendous effect on them so look after them:

♥ Eating whole, fresh, energy-rich foods as a matter of course will impact almost instantly on your general vitality and help harmonize your hormone production.

♥ Go organic too, as much as possible, to avoid poisonous insecticides and fertilizers which may throw your hormone balance and sabotage your health.

♥ Steer clear, as much as possible, of paste-forming 'dead' foods like biscuits, cakes, pasta and white bread containing refined flour, and go easy on foods loaded with saturated fats like chips and crisps. Cut right down on coffee, alcohol and drugs – they'll throw your endocrine system out of kilter.

♥ Get out in the fresh air every day – you're alive, you need light!

♥ Take some daily aerobic exercise too in the great outdoors: your lungs need air, your muscles need work, you need the high! It doesn't have to be hard work – it can be fun. Walking's fine – borrow someone's dog. Or do some sport. Or go dancing. Something that is purely, simply, gloriously for you to generate the endorphins that will make you feel wonderful. And sexy.

✻ ✻

The mind is hugely powerful. You've been given a magical body, full of life, singing with sexuality; with attention and care you can keep the amazing structure of your body fit and feeling good. It's the home of your mind and will give you optimum pleasure and contentment when, using your mind, you look after it.

Think positive to feel positive

When you're feeling happy, content or just calmly positive, you're well in spirit – a sign that your mind is on good form too, fit and healthy. It's easier to think clearly about all aspects of your life including your personal direction, friendships and any special relationships. Situations can be seen in perspective so that nothing is exaggerated or diminished unrealistically.

This all has a direct effect on your health. Problems are easier to cope with and healing speeds up. Even if your body is having problems in some way, your overall feeling is of well-being.

Another circle:

It's very similar to the sexual circle of response – the mind having a direct effect on the body. And the chemical or hormonal messenger system is at work too. Sceptics may laugh at the think-positive brigade, even though the results are plain to see in the increased well-being of body, mind and soul, but research has proved it isn't self-delusion. Positive emotions like love and hope can, just like thought, actually cause chemical reactions in the brain, producing substances like adrenalin, dopamine, endorphins and serotonin that help us keep fit and heighten our responses and moods. It's another cause/effect/cause circle.

The sexual impact of positive emotions

But the most exciting thing is that these hormones don't just make us feel better – directly and indirectly they lift our sexual awareness. The I-want-it factor sparks and soars. Your body suddenly feels worlds better and reminds you of its potential to feel sexy. You start thinking about sex more too and you're far more aware of sexual connotations in the world around you. Which comes first, body or mind? They encourage each other into being, and urge each other on. And, once the thought's there, the sexual circle starts spiralling aided and abetted by the feel-good hormones.

Read and Write Your Own Positivity

READ the situation to think positive

Register any negative feeling and identify it, as anger, hurt, jealousy, outrage, whatever, the instant you feel uncomfortable.

Empathize with the feeling. There's an immediate feeling of relief when you think – yes, I know how that feels and can see why it's come up.

Address the situation – the cause and your reaction. If your feeling is righteous, the cause needs attention. So consider what's wrong about it. If your reaction is over-the-top, look at that and think how much you reasonably need to tone it down or oust it completely. If it helps, think how you would advise a friend if they were negatively OTT about something.

Demonstrate this positive thought-pattern. If the feeling was justified, think what needs to be done, by you or whoever's responsible. Then take action to prompt positive change. If you realize there was no need for negativity, replace it firmly with a warm, positive thought.

WRITE your own script for a positive attitude

Willpower – you have it, so use it. Choose to view every situation in the most positive light possible. Don't think darkness, think light.

Remind yourself you're thinking positive as frequently as it takes. Break the negativity habit – kick it out of your life!

Initiate things to feel positive about. Look for the good all around you. Create more.

Tell yourself you and the world are wonderful. You are. It is. Yes there's potential for improvement but don't make perfection the enemy of the good. Appreciate it. Encouragement and praise work better than harsh criticism.

Enjoy your self, your life, your sexuality, your loved ones.

Paint your life story with *joie de vivre* in the colours you love.

> **Great sex – the sort you want – is one of the wonders of the world.**

Like many good and beautiful things, sexuality and lovemaking seem totally natural when they're functioning well – simple, easy and right. And it is 100 per cent natural to be at ease with your sexuality and to enjoy good sex. If your body is healthy, it's ready and waiting to let the sexual circles of response flow. The only go-ahead it needs to express your sexuality and let you luxuriate in great sex is your permission. The process will continue along with your willingness. And your awareness and appreciation of the wonderful feelings, physical and emotional, along the way encourage them to blossom, bringing more and deeper joy.

Fulfilment's the same – it's up to you to register your awareness of your sexuality and give it your full approval. Then you can live positively, happy to be a sensual, sexual creature, whether single or in a relationship; happy to have the ability to enjoy great sex.

Rejoicing in your sexuality – on your own or with a partner

Your sexuality is your awareness, recognition and delight in your body's sexual orientation, your sexual sensations and the way you feel about them. Alone or in a relationship, good sex is the result of resting easy in your sexuality, content with your gender, relaxed about your body, glad for your sexual feelings and confident in expressing them.

Enjoying sex on your own ... Solitary sex is a pleasant gift you make to yourself, one of the joys of life – and it can be great sex. You don't have to have a partner to luxuriate in your sexuality or to enjoy sex. Great sex is just as possible for you if you're single and celibate as it is with a partner. The key is self-esteem as it encourages you to give pleasure to yourself lovingly and accept it with joy. Awareness and appreciation of your sexuality foster a wonderful feeling of contentment and fulfilment, whether you're single or in a relationship, celibate or sexually active.

Or with a partner ... This is what many people think of as best sex – and certainly there's more variety of sensations, and a whole gamut of emotional side-effects when you're having sex with someone. But it is far, far more complicated. Your scope to enjoy sex is largely based on your psyche, and the minute you involve someone else there are all your feelings about them to contend with, plus their own mind-set on sex, and their feelings, approach and reaction to you.

Sex is so amazingly involved – how on earth can you manage to arrive at great sex? But Nature is kind – sex, when it's working well, happens naturally and joyously. All you need is to want it to be good (and if you're with someone for them to share the wish) and you can get there. The seven secrets make it easy and fun – just heavenly all the way. The potential for comfortable sexuality and great sex is there, within you, all the time – it's up to you to recognize it and embrace it. To say YES! – this is going to be a fantastic part of me and my life. Be glad – be joyous – sensuality, sexuality and great sex are priceless treasures and they're all yours.

With self-understanding and encouragement your ability to enjoy your sexuality more confidently, more surely, will grow and flourish. Be your own expert – on yourself, your life, your relationships and your amazing capacity for pleasure. Have fun exploring your sensual, erotic and sexual potential.

And let the seven secrets light your way to making joy a permanent fixture in your life ...

Part 2

Believing *in You*

Brilliant sex and joyful sexuality radiate from a wellspring of self-confidence and self-love

When you stride, or better still dance through life the energy you generate brims so full it powers your sexual awareness and your libido. You'll be able to use and relish the secrets of sensual sex and they in turn will recharge your confidence.

Hah – I can hear you saying – easily said! But how many of us can muster self-confidence on a constant basis, if at all? What about when it dips or plummets, or what if you've never taken off from a base of low or non-existent self-esteem?

OK, I know. Life isn't always rosy. Don't worry. Inspiration is always there. It just needs accessing, along with contingency plans to build – and/or re-build – your confidence as and when necessary.

Here is a kick-start statement. Learn it and repeat it whenever confidence wavers and threatens to sabotage your zest for sex.

> *I am the start and the flight and the resting place of passion.*

You are powerful, able and in control of *your* life, your sexuality, your sex-drive.

Yes, they go hand in hand with self-esteem, but self-esteem can be encouraged into vibrant life whatever your age; it can always be strengthened and, where necessary, repaired.

You and your self-esteem work with the secrets, with your senses – all of them, to give them life. And they too are rooting for *you* – for your self-confidence, your enjoyment of yourself – body, mind and soul.

As ever your mind is the motivating, driving force. The more you ponder the secrets, revelling in their possibilities, the more confident you'll become. It starts with a thought: Say it, think it:

▶ *I want the secrets to work for me.*

As you say it your interest sparks along with awareness and inspiration. Go on, say it aloud again:

▶ *I want the secrets to work for me.*

And then:

▶ *I'm going to use the secrets to improve my sex life, enjoy my body and be truly, amazingly sexually fulfilled.*

Thinking it, and backing up the thought by saying it out loud, sets your conscious and subconscious mind in action, generating the means to make it happen for you, unlocking blocks, seeking solutions to any puzzles or problems, forging the way to fundamental confidence in yourself and your ability to enjoy your sexuality and the most sensuous, deeply orgasmic sex.

Building Confidence So You Can Bring the Secrets into Your Life in All Their Glory

Now help your mind along some in your quest for confidence – whether it's a new idea for you, or something that needs topping up, often or occasionally, or something you'd just like to increase and benefit more from.

It helps to take a look at why your self-confidence isn't as strong as it could be and how that has a knock-on effect on your sexuality.

Often it's because our culture specializes in sabotaging self-esteem. Despite our supposed freedom, you may feel you've got to follow slavish fashions like breast implants and body piercing and, with a semi-starved body shape held up as the ideal, chances are you're not happy with your weight.

Families and friends and even partners don't always help much either – teasing's often compulsive, constant and damaging. Even if you're one of the fortunate ones whose parents helped you believe you're just fine the way you are, most likely you're not completely comfortable with and in yourself?

So get ready to throw off the self-dissatisfaction that's been foisted on you. Make a decision, right now, that you're going to go the other way. Accept yourself, your body, your character – the whole *you* as you really are.

It's the feeling of being a whole person – the real you – complete

You may have experienced this sublime feeling of personal and sexual completeness by chance when single, or in the early stages of a relationship, or since then but always intermittently, never as a constant factor. Or perhaps you've only dreamed of how it would feel. It's a place many don't arrive at, or can't often find, whether single or in a relationship. The sublime feeling of wholeness may seem uncatchably elusive.

And that can be the start of a dulling of sexual enjoyment. The high hopes you have for a thrilling sex life and/or deep, enjoyable sense of your sexuality dim if you can't depend on them. Good sex can soldier on for a while, but increasingly there's an ominous sense of struggle to keep the momentum going.

But you can keep the essential wonder of great sex and your joyous, confident sexuality in your life. And it's down to you – all the way.

Good sex isn't a work-out –
it's a mind, body and spirit experience

Everything we're taught about sex focuses on a path from desire through the arousal curve via pleasuring to the goal of satisfaction. Casual sex that's just out for the physical thrill may be just that – but it's like scratching an itch: no big deal and certainly not the dream you'd like to be a reality of your life.

The truth is that good sex, the fulfilling sort we really want if we're honest, isn't a one-way trip. It's a return journey via a circular route. And the starting point mirrors the blissful sexual aftermath where you feel complete. The starting point is you, but an at-home-with-yourself you.

For good sex to work its magic all or most of the time, and to stay an integral part of a relationship, it depends on you having high, sustainable self-esteem.

All the various meanings of sex, including the feeling of wholeness, may, through fortune and excitement and maybe a hit-and-miss chemical reaction, descend on you spontaneously, especially in a new relationship. But they won't keep coming to fruition together, if at all, unless *you* are together.

Forget looking to your partner to give you confidence. You can find confidence within yourself.

Forget the cliché that finding Mr or Ms Right will make you whole. You are already whole.

Forget the idea that a perfect partner will transform your life. You have the power to transform your life yourself.

Your life and your ability to enjoy happiness and best sex is within you, no one else can give it to you.

> *The key to the fullest appreciation of your
> sexuality is to be yourself and to like yourself.*

Then you'll be ready to accept someone else into your life, appreciate intimacy and let their sexuality complement yours.

▶ **When two individual people are each happy in their own bodies and souls they can come together and reach the stars.**

Fight fear – find yourself

Whatever the state of your self-regard, it can probably do with an uplift and needs regular maintenance. Our minds and personalities are a curious blend of strong and fragile. Just when we think we've got it all together and are stepping out in style – confident cool people – something happens and we trip up, sliding into a morass of confusion and terror that we're losing our grip. When self-doubt and anxiety set in it's bad news for your sexuality.

Face the fear by recognizing how fragile you are but also registering your innate strength. The worst may not happen and, if and when something dreadful crops up, it will be easier dealt with if you bring to it a fresh mind and spirit.

Remember – and this is the crux of self-esteem – that you are a capable person. Think of that as copeable. There's simply no point torturing yourself with insecurity and worry, stress and imaginary strain. If needed, you will deal with whatever trouble comes your way. Our minds have an amazing resilience if we don't sabotage their power with endless doubt and fret.

The minute you realize you are both vulnerable *and* strong, an astonishing thing happens – your self-esteem stops dangling you over a precipice above treacherous icy rivers of fear and lets you put down roots of self-confidence in firm ground.

Repeat these affirmations whenever self-doubt or downright worry lurks:

I am a capable person.

I can cope – I do cope with whatever life brings.

I am relaxed and free of anxiety.

I will state the logic of a situation and view it in perspective.

I will stress the plus points, the pros, the potential.

The more self-confident you are, the more you will enjoy life, the better your relationships will flow, and the more satisfying on the physical, emotional and spiritual planes your sex life will be. Inner well-being maximizes your potential to enjoy sex to the full.

In case you're a rebel and digging your heels in, I want to stress that you're doing this for *you*. Not for me or the writers of any books you may read about confidence or self-esteem, not for your counsellor, or even (except indirectly) your partner either. It's for you and your ability to be happy, for you and your sex life, for you and your sexuality.

▶ *Keep focusing on looking after your self-esteem.*
It's possibly the most important thing in your life and it
is certainly the most catalytic element of your sex life.

Build Your Self-Esteem –
Boost Your Sexuality

Most people see body image as the foundation of their self-
esteem, or lack of it. How you feel about the way you look
probably has a big effect on the way you view sex, feel your
own sexuality and relate to your partner. But chances are, like
most people, you're not 100 per cent happy about your body.

So let's look at the keys to changing your self-image first –
it will have a huge impact on your self-confidence and your
sexual confidence and enjoyment too. It's much much easier
to feel sexy when you feel attractive. Listen to me – you *are*
attractive. You're gorgeous, lovable, desirable. You are *you* –
and no one else in the whole world is the same as you. Isn't
that incredible? You are fantastic – inwardly and outwardly!

I can tell you the truth about your inner and outer beauty,
but hearing and believing it is up to you. Your choice.

Step by step, firm decision by firm decision and with gentle,
persistent practice, raise your self-esteem.

Just remember, and keep reminding yourself, that building
your physical confidence will have a great effect on your
sexuality and your sex life, both indirectly by increasing your
general self-esteem and by allowing you to relax and forget
what you look like when you're having sex.

Love yourself – like the way you look
The key is to start loving your body, every centimetre of it.
As you start to appreciate it, long-time prejudices about
your body, attractiveness and magnetism will tumble, one by

one, and you'll be amazed at how good the new physical confidence feels.

> *Make friends with your body and treasure it for it is your home and the safe haven, while on this earth, of your mind and soul.*

A daily ritual to start boosting and feeding your physical confidence and self-liking

This is good. So do it – do it for *you*.

1 Stroke yourself and watch (or if you're in bed at night just feel) your hand moving silkily over the surface of your skin. Watch or feel the shape of the flesh or muscle or bone beneath your hand. Marvel at the structure of the part of your body you're touching, and at your whole complex, marvellous form.

2 Say thank you to your body for looking after you. Be glad for your special shell.

3 Cup the first three fingers of your hands over your eyes and press very, very gently and hold them there for a minute, the palms of your hands gently covering your cheeks.

4 Say to yourself: 'I am at peace with this sweet face, these gentle eyes', and feel warmth and love, for yourself and all your loved ones.

5 Then glide your hands down the sides of your throat and down over your chest, your stomach, hips, thighs, calves, ankles and feet, ending with a gentle, lingering press against your toes.

6 If you are near a mirror, look at yourself in the glass and smile – or laugh – at your funny, dear face and send a wave of love to yourself. Say 'Perfect you're not, but special you are and I love you.'

Reinforce the growth of confidence with logic

Once self-acceptance is under full sail, your confidence in your natural attractiveness will speed ahead too.

Your appeal to your special loved ones, and indeed the world in general, has little to do with conventional beauty – and that's excellent because your magnetism for others can grow more vibrant as the years progress, in tandem with your ability to enjoy being you. Knowing this and being confident about yourself and your impact on others will charge your sexuality and your zest for life will soar.

Your looks, in the conventional attractiveness stakes, aren't important to your sexuality, but your self-image is, in all sorts of ways.

For one thing, to be up for sex on a regular basis with a long-standing partner you need to feel good about yourself. Self-confidence feeds libido – and your partner will pick up on it and feel good too.

Besides, to enjoy a wide range of sexual pleasure, approval of your body is a must.

So back up the last exercise, again on a daily basis, by looking after your body. Pamper yourself with good, healthy food; soothe your skin with lotions that smell and feel good; use make-up, jewellery, etc, if it pleases you and dress in clothes that make you feel great too. Get enough sleep, and adequate exercise to keep in reasonable shape. Watch out for too much stress – don't tax your system, care for it.

Begin, in other words, to feel the wonder of having such a structure, all of your own. And start to look after it better than ever before.

Take your time

Don't expect to change your perception of yourself overnight – it may take time. Let your mind work its magic. You want to be in tune with your body, you want to be glad to be inside it, so you've already set the process of change in motion. It may take you by surprise how quickly you start to feel good about yourself, or it may be a slow, almost imperceptible process but you will make friends with your body if you want to.

Your body is yours to look after as you will, to enjoy and to share at your will, no one else's. Enjoyment of all your senses and your sexuality is your choice.

▷ *Think self-esteem. Think sex. Think health.*

Your body is a precious part of your whole being. So, be good to yourself and think vitality and health – you'll automatically be including your sexual vibrancy.

Kicking the fear you don't match up

Take the fashionable idea of beauty with a pinch of salt and don't compare yourself with the media idea of physical perfection. How boring it would be if we all looked the same, but we don't – we are all different.

Open Your Eyes To Your Beauty

Make a list of the especially good points of your body: anything you think looks good or which others have complimented you on. Here's a checklist:

☐ Eyes   ☐ Neck .
☐ Ears   ☐ Shoulders
☐ Mouth   ☐ Chest/breasts
☐ Cheekbones   ☐ Hips and Bum
☐ Hair   ☐ Feet
☐ Skin   ☐ Legs

Maybe you haven't really valued all these parts of yourself before? Take a look at your list of plus points one by one, drawing out and accentuating your good feelings about each.

1 Look, for instance, at the shape and colour of your eyes, the curves or angles of your hips, the way the light falls on your back. Look at the strength of your legs and the beauty of their form.

2 Imagine you're looking with the eyes of a life-artist. See the sensuality of each 'good' feature.

3 Now do the same for the 'not so good' features: look for the beauty you may have missed – it may be hidden or simply unobserved:

4 Is there a way to improve the feature? Your skin, for example, might be transformed into smooth, clear beauty if you make a plan to look after it, inwardly and outwardly, with a healthy eating plan, a daily all-over massage with moisturizing lotion and aromatherapeutic oils. And the potential beauty of your shape can be maximized, again by feel-great eating and strategic exercise.

5 Finally, send a wave of love to each part of your body, 'good' or not and appreciate how precious it is to the whole you.

Whenever the impossibility of even competing, let alone matching up, gets you down or attacks the roots of your self- and sexual confidence, reflect on these two points:

Firstly, most images these days are idealized by technology. Just as the spinner of fairy tales could give the hero and heroine perfection at the touch of their pen, so can the air-brush lift skin imperfections and facial irregularities clean off the page or screen. Good camera work and clever make-up and lighting can also transform looks.

But nobody wants a relationship with a fantasy figure. We want real, honest-to-goodness partners who can be friends as well as lovers. Warmth of character, an ability to love and be loved, and emotional and practical generosity are far far more important than facial looks and bodily attributes.

Secondly, beauty doesn't make sexual confidence and appreciation any easier – in fact it can tangle the whole emotional scene, tying knots in the ability to be yourself and let yourself go.

Your attractiveness is your personality and your partner will love the way it shines through your expressions and movement, whatever form your bone structure and its covering take. Your body is the form in which you inhabit this world and through which, generally and sexually, you communicate with others. So cherish yourself with the loving care you deserve. It isn't narcissistic or vain, it's common sense.

Vitality allows your mind and body to link together and enjoy best sex. In Part 3, Chapter 7 mind, body and soul health is explored.

Building Your Emotional Confidence

If you're already confident in yourself, or know that you are ready and able to start building your confidence now, you may like to skip the next section. Otherwise, if you know in your heart there's something inside your heart and mind blocking confidence, read on.

Discovering what locked the natural development of your self-esteem

Take a look at where your fears and self-doubts originated. It could save you years of false starts and thwarted development.

And think of the benefits: confident enjoyment of your sexuality with the warm wonderful feeling of wholeness firmly attached.

If you realize a lack of self-esteem is having a profound effect on your sexuality, your sex life and your relationships, then the past needs to be faced and addressed. The old belief it took years to change deep-seated attitudes and 'blocks' has given way to a new realization. It doesn't have to take so long. With the help of a counsellor, you can break free of the chains that stretched back linking through the years and leaking uncertainty into your life. Counselling, once you find a good counsellor who you feel safe with and who works well with you, is a marvellous, life-changing experience. At its best it's inspirational, healing and confidence-building.

Two points to remember. You need to be ready and willing to work on yourself and start making positive change. And you need to feel comfortable and safe with your counsellor. Once you've found him or her, connect and enjoy the process of self-development – it's exciting.

Breaking Free of Old, Negative Patterns

When you feel fearful or unsure of yourself, grab a few minutes' peace and quiet on your own. Relax, and ask your mind to let you know where the feeling is coming from. Let your mind review the years in its own time. Just be still and calm and listen, aware that the answers will come to you in time.

You may find this doesn't happen at once. When we ask our subconscious to come up with something, it can take a while. The more you practise meditation (for more on meditation see Part 3, Chapter 7) or prayer, the faster the response is likely to be, but it's generally within 24 hours. It could be you'll wake up the next morning and think, 'Oh yes, of course, that explains it.' Or it may pop into your mind at any time of the day or via a dream or daydream.

If the emotion on discovering the sources of your low self-esteem is intense, only explore it further with a counsellor so that you can safely re-live the feelings. Think of how it feels in your body too: negative emotions always have a physical effect. It might be tightness across your back, an ache in your chest, a headache, tension in your neck, or a feeling like you'd been kicked in the stomach. Simply by stopping to look at the feelings – emotional and physical – in the spotlight of your full attention, you will dissolve their power to affect you any longer.

Finally, come back out of the feelings and ask God, or if you don't have a religion, the power behind the universe, or just simply ask, for peace. You need to do this to calm yourself after your search. Then consciously forgive those who stunted your development – whether or not they did it intentionally is their story. Now you can move on and neither they, nor anyone else, will ever have the power to undermine you again, for you are now on track and building your self-confidence.

As your self-esteem grows, you will increasingly sense your feeling of completeness and calm and begin to feel supremely safe in the knowledge that whatever life gives you, and whatever feelings you have, you can react appropriately in the best way.

Finding out who you are and learning to be yourself openly and unashamedly is the first step to prepare yourself for full enjoyment of sex – *best* sex. Now you can nurture a positive, welcoming attitude to sex, not just a pretence but a glorious gutsy YES! to your sexuality.

Part 3

The Seven Secrets of *Mind-Blowing Sex*

♥ ♥

Love your life and give it your best

The life within you and all around you holds much beauty and great promise. Give it the very best chance to give you what you truly want. Work with it, go with the flow of what's right for you. Give your sexuality your attention, your love. Give life a chance too and it will give you the world you want. Push out the boundaries of your capacity for happiness and joy. Ask your mind to explore, to enjoy, to let you celebrate the promise and the reality of feeling sexy, fulfilled, satisfied – mind-blowingly great!

Have fun, be passionate, be intense, be deep and calm and rich. Explore your emotions – their depth, height and width. Explore yourself and step-by-step build your confidence. Explore your relationship and its potential to be what you want. If, in doing so, you realize it isn't and can't be right, then use the mounting confidence to go forward in a better way and if that means splitting up, do so the kindest, fairest way possible.

The secrets are always there for you. Whether you're in a relationship or not, your appreciation of all your senses will help you, replenishing emotional energy, inspiring you to press on along the path that's right for you, and shining a light along the way for you to follow.

The secrets are your friends. Let them help you. They will enrich your sexuality and your life.

The First Secret:
The Power of Vision

♥ ♥

Your eyes are a bright window to your sexuality and the view outward and inward is profoundly clear and multi-dimensional. Through your sight you pick up and transmit an extraordinary amount of information and make a connection with others. The link is a potent helper and force in reading the world, those around you and especially your partner.

The moment our eyes met ...
The minute you see someone your brain assesses their appearance instantaneously and categorizes them. You have an immediate first impression. It's a complex chemical and emotional equation that no computer could begin to tackle. Initial sexual attraction is usually a visual response like this. Eyes are the first gateway, for most people, to fancying someone, and in the most extreme form they transmit the bolt from the blue that we call falling in love or, more cynically but realistically, lust. Pheromones, character, your inter-action,

compatibility, individual and couple mind-sets all come quickly to bear, determining the nature of any resultant relationship. In the beginning, the eyes have it.

There's the immediate 'eyes across a room' way
Your eyes meet and hold and move on, but you know your life has changed. You're spellbound. In love. You want to get to know that person. You feel as though you already do. The reaction that's occurred – is it emotional, or physical, or both? Whichever, one thing's for sure: it's set up a chain reaction in your body. You're interested sexually. You might use eye contact again to flirt and reassure each other of the energy that's sparked between you. But you don't need to. Every part of your body is hyped up with awareness that the person is there and your conscious and subconscious are going flat out to get you together. And it all started with a look.

At a slower pace, visual response to each other is still important, if not so earth-moving
Maybe instant attraction isn't your way. You could look at a woman or man and register no special interest. But then you get to know them more and find you like them. As friendship develops attraction can begin – you start seeing them differently. The more affectionate you feel, the more attractive their face and body seem. Gradually, as you begin to trust each other, you begin to look longer into each other's eyes; the exchanging and holding of the glance a sign of deepening feeling. Again, it's a powerful aphrodisiac: gazing into each other's eyes isn't so much about romance as about sex.

The Greatest Turn-On For Men – And Women Too?

Sight is a huge force in arousal too. Your looks turn each other on so accept your partner likes to look at you. Let go of self-consciousness by concentrating on their pleasure and yours as you take in the contours of their face and body with much affection.

The power of eye contact

Look deep into each other's eyes at any stage in an established relationship. Eye contact transmits energy: it can fuel lust and drive arousal or simply put you in touch with your innate sexuality.

We're not used to looking people in the eye in this culture. We drop our gaze if we make eye contact with strangers in the street. We tease friends and colleagues if we catch them gazing at us with a 'What are you looking at?' Or we worry 'What's the matter?' However close, relatives and friends may rarely look deep into each other's eyes and parents stop looking into their children's eyes once they're past the toddler stage.

It's natural to be frightened because we sense how powerful it can be when eyes meet and hold. And, just as some races are scared of the camera, we're scared of looking at each other, long and deep, because we fear losing something of ourselves.

Don't be frightened – think of the potential. Look deep into your partner's eyes – it's an intimate and energizing way of expressing your self and making contact with his or hers.

As well as being an instant way to connect at a deep level with them, you'll put your mutual attraction and arousal on fast-forward. And, once you relax about eye contact and go with the flow of energy, it feels great in itself.

Use your eyes. They are the window to your soul and using

them expressively will help others know and understand you. Deepen your understanding of them too, as you look into their eyes, and let the connection draw you closer.

Learning to use your eyes in social contact

The more confidently you use your eyes socially, the more relaxed you'll be in your sexuality.

1 Look into people's eyes as you speak to them. Notice how you shy away from eye contact. Break the habit. Practise looking the person you are speaking to in the eye – it will make you both feel good.

2 Practise holding the gaze of those you speak with. Everyone needs a rest from direct eye contact, but constant butterflying away makes you both unsettled. Make your point, or listen to theirs, with your eyes in contact and only then look away to collect your thoughts. In a group of people, share eye contact equally between them as you speak, and when someone else is speaking keep your eyes on their eyes.

3 With your eyes register interest in them and warmth towards them. Smile with your eyes. You know how you instinctively warm to people with sparkling, smiling eyes? Others will, just the same, to your expressiveness.

4 Respond to what they're saying with your eyes. Use the muscles all around your eyes to register your reactions so that they can see clearly how you're reacting. Whether you're agreeing, approving, disagreeing or shocked or amused – show it with your eyes before you get the chance to speak.

5 Be aware of the power of eye contact. Notice how you can draw the speaker to you with the attention of your eyes. The energy of your attention and awareness makes them feel good and sets up a rapport of mutual interest. It's powerful. It's all about *you* and your personal aura.

Remember, even when you're in company where there are no sexual undertones between the people, your own personal sexuality is nevertheless alive and kicking and dependent on you feeling good. Easy, relaxed sociability is part of that and so is a love of others.

The sexual impact of eye contact

In a relationship eye contact is the path to another dimension: it allows and energizes connection sexually and possibly emotionally and spiritually too. Even in a casual relationship, where you probably don't want to expose too much of your self, eye contact adds depth. Expressive eyes are the window to your sexuality and desire, they strengthen your sexual magnetism and, all the way, the pleasure you'll both feel.

It's something you probably do instinctively when you're in love but, months or years into a relationship eye to eye communication easily slips and can eventually cease altogether. Don't let it. Look into your partner's eyes, read their soul and let them read yours. Meet them, reach out to them, through your eyes.

Strengthening the sexual power of your eyes

1 Relax your body. You want to be with this person. Let your physical tension fall away. Feel the tightness across your shoulders and back and dissolve it. Loosen up – this is where you want to be.

2 Same with your eyes. Smile with them. Drop any tension.

3 Look into both of their eyes in turn, but don't keep switching – it's too distracting. Be aware, go easy and don't frighten them with too much intensity.

4 Feel your love and warmth towards them and let your eyes show your feeling.

5 Step up the sexual pace by moving your gaze from their eyes down to their mouth and back again.

6 Same again but now right down their body and, slowly, back up to their eyes. This is incredibly sexy for you and them. It can be an obvious come-on, or an innocent, unstudied sign of your sexual interest in them which will have just as positive an effect.

7 When you're making love make eye contact often and drink deep – register your pleasure with your eyes. Connect and fuse together.

Talk to your partner with your eyes. With your eyes you give each other the keys to your souls and your sexuality.

Soak Up Beauty and Turn On Your Sexuality

Beauty, noticed, expands into joy and becomes orgasmic ...

Your eyes are a conduit for your soul to joy. With them you soak up beauty and once you're used to absorbing beauty from all sorts of visual sources – art, the landscape, nature and the kaleidoscope of life – you'll begin to feel at one with inner pleasure, joy and ecstasy. It's an easy step from there to a consciousness of your sexuality. Just as the mind and body are inextricably linked on the physiological front, so is the appreciation of beauty linked to the pleasure and joy in your sexuality.

Understanding and tapping in to joy through your everyday vision is a simple but hugely effective way to find and deepen your sensuality and sexuality – your response to life's elemental energy.

Picking up on beauty and letting a response of pleasure

flood through you is a knack. If you're used to it that's great – if not, have fun learning. It will transform your sexuality too.

Two illustrations of this

John has worn glasses since his teens but remembers a time before that when he saw the world through a fog. 'I stopped looking at things and people,' he says, 'and just concentrated on getting from A to B safely. It became a habit not to look, which continued even when glasses gave me near perfect sight again.' But then he became interested in wildlife conservation and took to the hills with a local group. 'They were seeing things I completely missed – close by and in the distance. I started using my eyes to scan my whole field of vision and it was like a miracle. I was astounded by the variety of flora and fauna: it was like walking into a wonderland except I'd always been there and just hadn't noticed. Now I do. I still have to consciously practise opening my eyes to the beauty – but I do, all the time and not just in the countryside but at work and at home. My girlfriend says I'm the most sensually sexy man she's known, but she doesn't know this is a new me. The joy of discovering the wonder of my sight has turned me on to all my other senses too and sex is fantastic now.'

Meg found joy in her sensuality and sexuality when she started drawing and painting. Like John, she began to see the world around her in far greater detail and through her portraits and life studies she became much more aware of the people in her life and their feelings and character. 'I realized I often hadn't really noticed them,' she says. 'But now I pause to take in their expression and their individuality. I can see the depth of my partner and it's given me the confidence to open up to him. We're far closer as a result. It's been like learning a new language and now I can communicate much more fluently and intimately – emotionally and sexually.'

Practise opening your eyes to an awareness of beauty with this exercise and each time you're struck by the wonder of something, follow it by paying attention to the way it heightens sensitivity to your general sensuality.

1 Look around you and choose something that catches your eye and appeals. It could be as simple as, for instance, a smooth round stone.

2 Think about why you like it – the colour, shape, meaning, texture?

3 Enjoy it and let the feeling sing.

4 Wonder about its origins. Imagine it on the floor of the ocean where it was ground into shape by waves and sand.

5 Start to devote the same awareness to anything you see in the landscape around you that attracts you. Look for appeal, then sense it.

6 Look at people: the way their expressions unfold, the texture of your partner's skin and the way the light falls on it as she or he moves. See the beauty, the wonder – feel the joy. Connect in love of this amazing world and your incredible bodies.

Awareness of beauty and your response to it awakens your own creativity, gives you zest for life and highlights consciousness of your sexuality too. You feel whole and miraculously, vibrantly at one with your sexual dynamism. Using your vision to link with beauty is vibrant and joyful.

Whether you choose to make this connection with your sexual self or not, the beauty connection deepens your intimacy with your capacity for deep sensual pleasure and an ecstatic response. Noticing beauty regularly – it's all around you so look and see and enjoy! – paves the way for easy orgasms and teaches you a lot about climax, for joyous appreciation of beauty is similar to the ecstasy of sex.

It's that Oh, that's amazing! feeling that goes right through you like an arrow of delight, leaving a trail of pleasure that radiates through your whole body.

So although on the surface glimpses – or floods – of joy through appreciation of visual beauty may be far removed from sexy thoughts or physical sensations, they can be a direct line to your sex drive.

What is and isn't beautiful is a very personal thing and it's true that 'beauty is in the eye of the beholder'. But this individuality provides a rich seam of oneness: the sense of self that is imbedded in self-confidence and allows you to find fulfilment in your sexuality, whether single or in a relationship.

The eyes see – the mind notices – awareness jolts through you – there's a chemical reaction – endorphins flood your body – you're more aware of beauty – you look

The Joy of Colour and Its Impact on Your Sexuality

Feast your eyes on colour for it will feed your soul, your sex drive *and* your ability to feel and transmit pleasure.

Colour has a powerful effect on your moods and can heal and inspire you. It's also a sexual catalyst, directly or indirectly, depending on the colour and shade. If, like many, you're not in the habit of noticing or paying much attention to colour and its effect on you, don't worry. As with beauty, you can learn to appreciate its blessings and use it beneficially to intensify and even spark sexual experiences.

Looking at colour and sensing what it means to you is like tuning in to a new wavelength. If you've never thought much about colour, try this questionnaire to find out where you are in the colour stakes. Then you can develop your colour sense and use it to intensify and harmonize your sexuality and relationships.

COLOUR AND YOU

❤ Is colour an important element in your life?

❤ Do you know your favourite colours?

❤ Do you buy clothes with them in mind?

❤ Do they feature prominently in your home?

❤ Do you know why you like them?

❤ Do you know how they affect you?

❤ Do you understand the mood-altering and sense-intensifying qualities of all the colours?

If you score seven yes-es read the next section anyway – you may learn something extra. If you score less than seven yes-es it's imperative to read on – it's time colour lit up your life.

Colour is charismatic and compelling

Taking an interest in the impact of colour on you and your life is healthy, sensual and fun. A love of colour is a sure sign of a passionate person, and developing your affinity with colour will strengthen your self-confidence and give you zest in sex, love and life.

So think of colour as a friend and mentor, from now on. Don't say, 'I've no colour sense.' Except in the rarest of ophthalmic conditions, everyone has the ability to gauge and appreciate colour.

To get you going, find out what the different colours mean to you.

Take a look around you now. Which colours shout at you immediately? List them. Now think and decide which ones you like most – put them into order of preference. Then start at the top – favourite first, and think, or rather feel, why it is that you like, or don't so much like, each one. How do you respond, mind and body, to each one? Your list will probably be completely different from mine – you have a unique perception of colour.

Yellow My study walls are the colour of clotted cream, the curtains a brighter sunshine yellow. There's a yellow bowl, a yellow book cover and, looking outside, a field literally buttercup yellow. Yellow makes me feel bright and happy. On the physical plane I can sense it on the back of my neck, as though it's helping me hold my head high.

Green Emerald green outside. It draws my eyes the whole time. It's the colour that my soul responds to, suggesting renewal and life.

Brown Natural woods – an oak beam over the window, a natural pine door and outside, pine cladding on the outbuildings and a weathered pine gate. The colour relaxes me – it's gentle and soothing.

Bright Pink A plumie pen top and a lush floribunda rose design on a giant mug make only tiny splashes of colour in my field of vision but lift my spirits high. The colour sings to me at the top of my head. It's a starry, pithy note.

There are heaps more colours, all around me as I work, but

these are the ones that reach out, calling: 'Look at me, look at me. I'm affecting you every instant!'

Colour, passion and sex

Tuning in to the impact colour is having on you at any time is to touch base with your sensuality in a very direct way. Colour is blatant and pressing. It's all about passion for life and passion for life is a must for great sex.

Even if you're working in drab surroundings, get in touch with the greys and buffs – what do they say to you? It may not be all gloom and doom: neutrals can have a levelling or calming effect on you and that's just as sensual in its own way.

Appreciate any colours around you that you really love or respond positively to. None there or only one or two? Then introduce them. It's such an easy way to bring rays of joy into your life and they'll light up your sensuality.

* *

NOT SURE WHAT YOU LIKE?

Learn with these steps:

- ♥ Look
- ♥ Use your eyes
- ♥ Learn about your response to colour just as you did beauty
- ♥ Feel your response
- ♥ Take your time
- ♥ Register your response
- ♥ Learn it for future use

* *

Mystics tell us we all vibrate – every particle within us, our whole being, and our auras. Every colour has its own special vibration too, which interacts with our body's vibration. In addition, our brains react chemically and emotionally to colour.

Physical or metaphysical, the way you react to every shade in the spectrum is unique to you and some of those reactions will be especially powerful, even life-transforming.

Gathered from a wide variety of healers and artists, these are some observations on the qualities of colour. But again, you may have very different ideas and besides, most of us are influenced by fashion and susceptible to change. Above all colour is fun – a wonderful blessing in our lives.

Pink is the colour of love and kindness, romance and goodness. It's a warm, soft, gentle-on-the-eye colour. Too much pink, though, may be cloying. So in relationships, tone down the sweetness with other colours.

Turquoise and aqua – the sea colours – combine the silky cool qualities of green and blue. They can wash through you with sensuousness so, if you love them, they're a good choice for bedrooms.

Red is famous as the colour of passion and vitality. Use it to flood yourself with energy and fill yourself with courage and flair. Red can be a healing colour too: it's therapeutic for the fluent circulation of blood and restores a feeling of vitality. But beware, red is also the colour of anger and rage. Don't use it when it might exacerbate an already bad mood or a potentially explosive situation; steer clear of it and use soothing or illuminating colours instead.

Blue is astonishingly healing and calming. Sunset sky blue, denim and navy are the most potent emotionally. Blue is also the elemental relationship colour. It's attractive to both sexes because it's the colour of communication and creative and emotional expression. It's the colour of joyous dance, art and music.

Orange is the colour of fruitfulness. Creativity and sexuality are complemented and inspired by orange. It's also a source of joy and a cushion for your inner child – a vibrant, joyous, pulsating colour.

Yellow sharpens the mind. It's a great colour for a working environment as it keeps you alert; especially good if you're under pressure, for instance, revising for exams or working to a deadline. It's a joy-making colour: try to stay down when you're wearing yellow or sitting in a predominantly yellow room!

Violet is the spiritual colour – it helps you settle into meditation or prayer. It helps you reach other dimensions too – your healing self and your sexual self.

White and pale neutrals like oat and silver are sensual colours. They bathe you with light and flush negativity out of you, allowing warmth and attraction to initiate desire. But beware of using them exclusively – without the spark of other colours they may remain too cool for comfort.

Black is good for sinking into, so it's a sensuous, sexy colour. But don't make your whole colour world black – not for nothing do people talk of black moods. Beware of too much grey as well. It's fine if used as a foil to throw other colours into the limelight, but on its own it can bring your spirits down, down, down.

Green despite its association with jealousy, is often a heart-warming, revitalizing colour – good for circulation and therefore good for your whole sexual system.

Choosing colours to expand your sense of sex

As you get to know your colour sense 'your' colours will speak to you more often, more deeply. Let them colour your life and make a statement about you to others. They provide an easy, delightful way to express your character, vitality and creativity. Use them, too, in your sexuality.

1 Think of the sex in your life: of your sexuality generally if you're not in a relationship, or of your memories of past sexual encounters or relationships, or, if you have a partner now, of the sex you share together.

2 Be aware, as you're thinking of sex, what colours are passing through your mind simultaneously. Shut your eyes. Think sex, think colour. Remember the colour(s) that predominate. Chances are the shades are of the same hues as your favourites. if not, perhaps they should be added to your personal colour spectrum. Register the colours you've subconsciously associated with sex so that you can use the next section effectively to enhance your sexuality and sex life.

Now take the fast lane to mind-blowing sex ...

The Ultimate Power of Your Mind's Eye – Visualization

Visualization is potentially a creative process: it opens up your mind to blissfully sensuous sex and frees your body to join forces and manifest the pleasure you want whenever you want.

It works in a series of ways each valid and valuable in its own right as a complement to your sexuality and, together, capable of transforming your sex life.

First of all it relaxes you, then it floods you with sexual awareness. This triggers a charge of energy and inspires you.

You know you're ready to enjoy sex and will be able to in full, mind-blowing measure.

Visualizing relaxation

To be able to let go of tension and relax is a must for great sex. It's about losing yourself in your senses and the awareness of your emotional and physical responses. Then you drop a level in consciousness so that you can sink into the sensuousness of sex. That way arousal and, in time, orgasm take you over as naturally and blissfully as if you were flying, supported by clouds of gossamer down.

Follow this technique for visualizing relaxation and once you've learned and practised the knack you'll be able to skip the stages and drop straight into relaxation, no matter the state of your day.

1 When you've time to take half an hour or so on your own, make yourself comfortable, sitting or lying down, close your eyes and for a few moments concentrate on your breathing. Extend each breath in and out, letting the transition move on as seamlessly as you can and deepening your breathing so that your stomach moves as well as your chest.

2 Now start to release tension and the day's happenings with each out-breath, and as you breathe in, each time, see and feel yourself taking in calm and peace.

3 See that for the moment nothing matters but this – your relaxation.

4 Think about a place that represents relaxation to you. It could be somewhere you really do know well or an imaginery oasis of calm. Maybe a green valley where you feel utterly at one with nature? The valley welcomes and holds you safely. What's your peaceful, safe place? See it in your mind. Feel. Be there.

5 See yourself, feel yourself, becoming totally relaxed and calm. Nothing else matters. This is for you. You are at peace.

6 When you're ready to come back to the here and now, register the picture of your place and the feeling inside yourself of being there, so that you can remember it well and revisit it whenever you want.

7 Now think about your breathing once again and, as you take an in-breath, visualize that you are bringing peace and relaxation and inner calm with you into your everyday life and this moment now as you come back. Press your heels, or the soles of your feet, depending whether you are sitting or lying down on the floor. Then touch something solid around you with your hands to ground yourself and come gently back into the moment.

A short cut to instant relaxation when you're about to, or already, making love

1 Remember the feeling when you were in your quiet place. See yourself there, be there.

2 Focus on your shoulders, or any other part of you that you tense when you're tense.

3 Let the tension drop away, just as you did in your quiet place.

4 Let peace flood over you. Drop down a level in consciousness.

5 Know that you are deeply relaxed and ready to engage. Connect with your partner and give yourself fully to the pleasure of building arousal.

6 Breathe deeply in and as you breathe out look into the eyes of your partner, giving them, in your mind, the ability to arouse you.

Visualize great sex – have great sex

However relaxed and willing your mindset on sex, if your or your partner's technique is somewhat limited or you've got into the habit of following a more or less set routine, the earth isn't going to move. Even if you reach climax, it won't be the mind-blowing culmination of physical and emotional pleasure that you'd naturally much prefer.

No need to settle for less than you want. Use visualization to get your mind confidently leading your body to true fulfilment.

Visualization is about changing your mindset and bringing a totally positive approach to your sexuality into being. Give yourself at least half an hour for this exercise and enjoy:

1 Lie or sit comfortably and use the relaxation technique given in full above, or breathing deeply, imagine yourself walking up steps.

2 Feel yourself losing tension as you climb and once you're settled into the rhythm of walking up stairs, see yourself reaching the level you wanted and stopping.

3 Look around you and see yourself in a simple setting with your favourite colour predominating. Be aware of your intrinsic sexuality and feel glad to be you, glad to be a woman or man.

4 Know – believing and accepting it – that you are absolutely in touch with your sexuality and capacity for sexual joy.

5 Know, and decide to re-affirm this regularly, that you are free and glad to celebrate your gender and your oneness with life and love, today and always.

6 Know that your sexuality is your friend, your support and part of your wholeness. Understand that your sexuality will never betray you for it's at one with your goodness and truth.

7 Give yourself permission to enjoy your sexuality. Say to yourself: 'This is mine to enjoy.'

8 Feel the rush of warmth and joy flooding upwards from the middle part of your body through your chest and spine to your shoulders and head.

9 Pause quietly.

10 Breathe deeply again, and as you release the third breath say to yourself, 'My sexuality is the greatest gift, thank you.'

11 Come back into real-life focus and ground yourself as before.

You Are Free to Fly

Your sexuality is a part of you, yours to explore as you discover more about your own emotional and physical wishes and needs. You are a whole person and it is your right to enjoy your sexuality in yourself and, if you are in a relationship, to have deeply fulfilling, joyous sex with your partner.

Life, light and sex

We – our bodies and our minds – love light. It lets us use the power of vision and it's an essential for physical health too. Our purpose is to grow, so live in the light as much as possible, physically, emotionally and spiritually. That way your sensuality and sexuality will flourish and feel wonderful.

* *

USING LIGHT – A RECIPE

Physically: Make sure you get outside in the daylight every day
for at least half an hour, longer whenever possible. Even in winter,
wrap up warm and go for a walk. Look up at the sky (shielding
your eyes from the direct glare of the sun) – you will immediately
feel livelier, and more in touch with your sexuality as a result. The
light around you will also lift your mood and strengthen your sex
drive.

See the light with your eyes and visualize it flooding your body
with energy and inspiration.

Regularly, when indoors, pause for a moment (that's all it
takes, I promise) to visualize yourself in the light again.

And whenever there is a problem between yourself and
your partner, imagine light illuminating it and your minds, so that
you can see the solution in clarity and the confidence you need
to right it.

* *

▶ *Empower your sexuality with the energy of light*
for it's inextricably linked to love and life.

The Second Secret:
Fantasy, You and a World of Pleasure

❤ ❤

Fantasy is startlingly orgasmic proof of the mind's power to spark and feel desire. It provides instant access to a world of erotic stories and pictures, and the most deeply sexual and sensual feelings. A more enticingly vivid virtual-reality than any computer could ever hope to summon. Your imagination is there at your beck and call, ready and waiting to switch on and fire your sexuality.

How amazing that we have this ability to step into another world, whenever we wish, and experience at first hand any pleasure we desire – even if we've never dreamed or heard of or experienced it before. How wonderful that we can invite and allow our mind pictures to translate into real, here-and-now physical and sexual sensations, initiating or intensifying desire, arousal and satisfaction along the way. And it gets easier and better with practice as you get used to fantasizing by using your mind.

If you're thinking, 'Well I haven't much imagination,' don't worry – it may be dormant or suppressed but it only needs freeing up.

Your fantasy life is another dimension and yours to use as you will. If you wish to keep it entirely to yourself, not even letting your partner in on it, you can. No one can read your mind. He or she will, of course, notice the effect of it in your emotional and physical response. Your partner couldn't fail to notice as you'll automatically step up a gear. But he or she will assume it's entirely down to him or her and will be delighted.

That's fine. With your pleasure expanding so richly it's good if your partner's enjoyment increases too. Be glad for yourself, for your partner and for your relationship. Then stand by for the next exciting development.

Once your fantasies unleash your ability to let go, you'll soon get used to enjoying every moment of lovemaking. Your arousal curve will become free of tension or reservation.

Then, instead of relying on the fantasy to fuel the pleasure, you'll be able to transfer the power to your partner. Their body, their touch, their movements – everything about them and their lovemaking can turn you on as certainly as the fantasy. With practice, you can make your partner the focus of your pleasure during or at the end of lovemaking as you wish. The fantasy of pleasure will become the most fulfilling reality.

But we're jumping ahead here. Go softly and slowly: it takes time to tune in to your fantasy world so well that you can step easily back and forth to the reality of your lovemaking. But that stage will soon come. In the meantime, enjoy the learning process – it's fun; it's all about pleasure.

So what is it like to set your mind free and feel the pleasure before it's backed up by or translated into physical touch and stimulation?

You've probably already experienced fantasy: think back

through teenage daydreaming or desire sparked by a crush or chance attraction. Live those feelings again; it will help your ability to fully appreciate sexual pleasure and joy. Recall any erotic dreams you've had too, where feelings for your story's hero or heroine drive your body to arousal and you wake on the verge of or in the throes of intense pleasure and orgasm?

That's what you're aiming for in your erotic fantasies. The translation of the (day)dream into physical, sexual stimulation.

Think sex – whatever sort of sex you want. Good, lustful, earthy, sensuous sex. Or romantic, tantalizing, sensitive, in-love sex. Whichever you're happiest with. The choice is entirely yours. Think sex (go on – give yourself permission) and you won't even have to try for arousal.

Uninhibited, your body will respond automatically. A chain of reaction will shoot through your nervous system to switch on the pleasure centres of your body, heightening sensitivity and flooding your erogenous zones with pleasure.

At the same time your mind is automatically reacting too, releasing adrenalin and other feel-good chemicals to heighten the pleasure and joy and mix energy and relaxation in precisely the right amounts for effortless, exquisite climax, whenever you're ready.

> ▶ *Fantasizing* can be a wander through erotic thoughts and images, gently searching for new ideas that turn you on, stirring emotions and physical sensation by happy chance rather than choice. Or your erotic daydreaming can be far more than a gentle amble through haphazard thoughts. It can – with you firmly at the controls – be a constructive and even programmed creative process.

You can write your own fantasies but if imaginary or fictional scenes don't spring into life don't worry, it's fine to use memories.

So think of the sex you had with previous lovers, or the best sex you and your partner have enjoyed. Remember your earliest times together. Many people report the excitement of sex with a new partner gives them easy, fast orgasms but later, once the first heady phase of the relationship is over, they're not stirred to anything like the same passion. So in your fantasy re-visit the best, the most exciting and/or the wildest erotic moments you've shared.

▶ *Remember. Feel again. Let the memory play all over again. Feel the sensations.*

♥ Home in on specific, one-off experiences.

♥ Re-live the various feelings of arousal and pleasure and satisfaction throughout your life.

♥ When did you first get turned on, kissed, petted?

♥ Think back to your first full experience of sexual pleasure. (I don't necessarily mean when you first had intercourse, but when you first enjoyed it or began to appreciate the sensual possibilities and potential.)

♥ If you climaxed, go back to that memory too.
Experience it again in your mind.
Feel the sensations.
Remember and bring them to the front of your mind to call on again, instantly, whenever you want – during masturbation or when you're having sex.

▶ *Mind wants. Focuses. Explores. Body connects. Reacts. Responds.*

▶ *Thought. Feeling. Touch. Mind. Fantasy. Reality.*

With a little enjoyable practice you will be able to pick and choose which fantasy, and even which precise part of it, you want to step into at any given time.

The impulse to have sex always starts in the mind. It's all about willingness and imagination. Fantasy takes both and you can encourage both into your mind and your life.

No imagination or you feel it's blocked? Don't worry – you can free it

You have a vivid imagination alive and well inside you and just itching to be allowed to light up your sex life.

Understanding why it's locked in is the first step to freedom.

What happened to your imagination? Sadly teachers often feel they have to squash their pupils' daydreams to get work done. And parents sometimes confuse a vivid imagination with dishonesty and disapprove it into oblivion. Any sexual element would have doubly horrified them. Terrified you'd attract or seek sexual attention far too early, they curbed it a touch too strongly. Or maybe it simply got crowded out – kids can be so busy with extra lessons, after-school activities and homework, not to mention busy social lives, that they just don't have time to dream.

Or perhaps you're frightened of unleashing some dark aspect of yourself you won't be able to control? That's understandable. If your carers were negative about daydreaming or romanticizing, they'd have given you, as a hugely impressionable youngster, the worrying impression that sexy thoughts and feelings were demons and your imagination a dangerous monster which lands you unceremoniously in serious trouble.

Once you see where your imagination fell, or was driven out of your life, you can pick up the pieces and encourage it back to life. Like most creative processes, the knack for bringing it into vibrant being comes when you give it the opportunity – so deliberately give yourself permission to fantasize the first few times. Soon it will come naturally and so, every bit as naturally, will you.

Fantasy is often likened to a garden in the mind – hence the title for Nancy Friday's classic book: *My Secret Garden*. It's a good analogy – fantasizing is like being in an amazing garden packed with endless varieties of sensual pleasures. Think sex and you can have sex – any way you want. Think a seductive story and you're the hero or heroine of your dreams. Think of yourself thrilling to any pleasure from vaguest notion to heart's desire and there you are, experiencing it. And being turned on: unmistakably physically sexually, heart-speeding gloriously aroused.

Fantasy is for *you*. Your friend, your guide, your follower.

Soon you'll be able to use your imagination at any time to spice up or trigger pleasure. It's useful at any stage of masturbation or during sex with your partner when it's just not happening for you. Fantasy lets the happening begin. Fantasy can be a pure first creation of pleasure, or a brightening of existing pleasure.

Stepping Into a Sexual Fantasy

For women Start familiarizing yourself with fantasy on your own – it's much easier that way at first. Maybe you're completely new to fantasizing, or haven't yet used it to enhance sensation or unlock elusive desire, arousal or orgasm. Either way it's a skill that's lying dormant and easily awakened and practised.

Learning the knack

Give yourself permission to enjoy fantasizing as a means of enhancing the pleasure you get from your own sexuality and from having sex.

2 Still stalling? Think this through: there is absolutely no reason you 'shouldn't' fantasize. You don't lose control of your thoughts – you can fantasize exactly what you wish. At any time if an uncomfortable thought comes into your mind, you can decide not to continue with the thought and change the picture accordingly. Your fantasy is totally your own. Relax – you are safe – you are entirely in your own hands.

3 Find yourself a time and a place where you are private and won't be interrupted. Your own bed is wonderful if you have the house to yourself or know the shut door will be respected. Otherwise a warm bath with the door locked behind you is better.

4 Lie down, get comfortable, and very gently feel your clitoris, directly if you like it that way, or just above through the hood.

5 Let your hand rest there quietly, with the heel of your hand or a finger pulsing gently, rhythmically and slowly. The aim is for this to be a background feeling, not a touch to expressly stimulate you into arousal – that's the fantasy's job.

6 Now take a look into your mind to see if there is a story waiting for you. Perhaps there is something – a person, an idea, a past event, that has always felt erotic? Sink into it and be in the feeling again. Weave it, and yourself, into a story around it.

7 If nothing comes to mind after a minute or two, use a book of erotic writing and read a paragraph here and there at random until a story interests you. You'll feel it instantly in your mind and your clitoris. Stop 'grazing' through the book and settle to read the story through.

8 Rememember any bits that particularly interest or excite you – 'store' them in your memory for future sessions.

9 If the story turns you on, or suggests an idea that you can elaborate in your mind, allow yourself to flow with the eroticism, the sexiness.

10 Now tune in to your physical sensations as you continue to read or view the story or idea in your mind.

11 Notice how not just your clitoris but the whole pubic area to both sides and above is feeling charged with pleasure and a feeling of wanting sex, wanting more. Use a vibrator if you have one, or try moving your wrist against the pubic area and vulva – always gently but as firmly as feels good.

12 Notice how the intensity of your feelings as your interest in the story grows, pacing the growing sensation in your vulva and clitoral area.

13 With your other hand stroke or gently squeeze your nipples and any other erogenous zones you find particularly arousing.

14 As the story climaxes, allow yourself to come too, if you're ready. Just schmooze along with it and you will, quite naturally. Or you might like to hold back from the final trip over the arousal curve into orgasm and slip back a way to let the build-up of pleasure happen all over again.

15 At the same time go back to the beginning of the part of the story where it started to turn you on and read it again as you let the sensations around your clitoris intensify again.

16 Do this as many times as you like – the edging back from climax and re-experiencing of mid-way arousal strengthens the sexual electricity and, when you decide to go ahead and let yourself come, it will probably be a far more powerful orgasm than if you let it happen the first time you imagine the fantasy.

17 When it happens, at the first sign of the orgasm overtaking you, lift your mind instantly from the fantasy to the sensations and enjoy the pure, unadulterated physical joy.

For men It's usually assumed that men automatically know how to fantasize and masturbate and have both down to a fine art. But most of the men who've talked freely and honestly with me say that sure, they fantasize as they masturbate, but it's very much a case of the instant gratification of a soft-porn fantasy coupled with as quick a 'wank' as possible. Although this is fine as the quick-relief mechanism it's used for, it isn't going to do much for the quality of your sex life on your own or with your partner.

You can learn to use fantasy to enhance your sexual confidence and pleasure. Practise masturbating on your own and develop the art of fantasy. Here are some ideas to explore.

1 As in the 'for women' section above, find a place where privacy and warmth are assured so that you can relax and take your time. It's important to be comfortable so lying on something soft is probably best.

2 Forget the instant-fix fantasy. Instead let your mind, as you take hold of your penis, explore and rest on something you've found erotic. It could be something explicitly sexy like an untried situation or position – or something that might mean nothing to anyone else but which turns you on powerfully: maybe the scent of your partner, an abstract painting that fires your imagination, or anything beautiful that touches your soul.

3 Dwell on the eroticism it stirs in you – live in the sensations, emotionally and physically, and at the same time, as you masturbate, move your hand in a different way from your normal method.

4 Vary your hold – the position of your hand, the rhythm, the speed, the grip. Try moving sideways as well as up and down, gently twisting.

5 The point isn't to come quickly; it's to tune your physical sensations to the pictures and feelings of eroticism playing in your mind.

6 Now let your mind move into a more physical, sexually sensuous mode. Focus on your sensations – how your thoughts and feelings are affecting every part of you.

7 Touch yourself – massaging, kneading, stroking – in other places. See how it complements and maybe heightens arousal. Take time to enjoy.

8 As in the 'for women' section, let your arousal ebb and flow as you alternate masturbating and relaxing. Re-experience the fantasy or expand it as you like. Alternate between urgency and being content to delay. Just stopping the action of your hand may be enough to keep your arousal curve from escalating into climax, but if you're worried that you're too close to the point of no return squeezing firmly just under the head of your penis will backtrack arousal until you're ready to go forwards again.

9 Stop, start, tantalize, enjoy. Eventually, when you're ready, instead of retiring from the final over-the-edge of the arousal curve into climax, go with it, letting go into orgasm – fantasy and physical sensation fusing in a meltdown of ecstasy.

And with your partner If your compatibility's proven and the early infatuation is metamorphosing into love and/or friendship, you have the chance to weave a sexual rapport so rich and satisfying you are deeply, powerfully, sensually together for as long as you want to be. Fantasy, at any stage of a relationship's growth, is a wonderful ally – a treasure of a gift both for your individual selves and your relationship.

1 Ask your partner about his or her fantasies. If they seem shy of talking about them, nudge them along a little. If they start to open up fine, but otherwise leave it. Not everyone wants to share their fantasy life and either way it's fine.

2 Suggest, lead, guide but every step of the way watch the reaction and don't edge forwards unless you know they're with you and not backing off. Aim to spark their interest and build on it.

3 But provided you're both happy about it, you'll find divulging your fantasies exciting.

4 Take turns to tell the other the story that drives you wild. Or tell them their favourite fantasy or have them tell you yours. It can be really erotic to hear something so personal to you coming from your partner's lips.

5 How about making a fantasy reality? If it's possible within the context of your relationship, or could be with a little make-believe, it's fine to re-enact a scene that turns you on. (Again though, only if you both want to; it's fine to say no if it's not your thing.)

6 If you go ahead don't worry if role-playing feels clumsy at first – any embarrassment soon fades if you concentrate on the fantasy and enjoying it. Encourage each other by openly showing how much you're enjoying it. Let go, get into the spirit.

7 Even if you don't want to act out fantasies, you can still experience the settings to complement the mind pictures. Find the sand dunes you've dreamed of, join the mile-high club, buy some black satin sheets – whatever you want!

8 Have fun: laugh together, later, about your fantasies and the wild effect they have on you.

9 If you're acting out the sexual experience of your fantasy, be directive with each other, down to the last detail, with demonstration or clear description. Always be positive – steer away from saying something's wrong, say 'this is how' and show them. You'll both be especially sensitive if you're fantasizing together.

Having it all – the warm sexy comfort of a relationship and the thrill of the chase

Fantasy lets you have it all. Let's admit it, we like the excitement of the chase, the thrill of satisfying new lust, the romance of falling in love – it's brilliant. But there comes a stage when you don't want to keep playing the field eternally – you want the chance to develop love and experience deeper, lasting emotions as well as hot sex. Or perhaps you meet someone so special you want to pledge fidelity.

Fantasy lets you have both the fulfilment of committed love and the passion of in-love. The great thing about your imagination is that all those magic thrills don't have to disappear from the equation when you settle down with someone. The comfort of familiarity factor can exist, paradoxically, side by side with as many exotic and varied affairs as you wish. Your mind is yours to involve you in the dramas of your dreams while luxuriating in the closeness and love you and your real-life partner share.

And with a huge bonus, as well as ousting any chance of boredom in a regular relationship, fantasizing will transcend even the instant arousals and spontaneous orgasms of the early relationship.

Won't fantasies come between us?

This may be a very real and understandable fear for you and your partner. Sure, either of you could get into such a habit of fantasizing that it became an obsession or a fetish. Like any source of pleasure, you might want more and more to the exclusion of your mutual connection when you're having sex.

So talk it through. It's good to be wary of any habit that could threaten to take you over. Remember, you are at the controls and can use fantasy purely to enhance and complement your personal and shared sexual pleasure and satisfaction.

What if fantasy arouses jealousy or uncertainty?

Get fantasies into perspective – neither of you really wants your wilder fantasies to come to life. They are sensual enhancers, that's all – imaginery spices to light up existing sensations and emotions. You wouldn't want to depend on them for sensory existence, any more than you would want to eat salt or curry powder. Fantasies add extra lustre to the precious gold of your sex life – they are not a substitute.

How to use your fantasy without your partner knowing

Fantasize discreetly if you or your partner prefer it that way.

1 As you are arousing each other, every now and then take the focus off your partner and concentrate on *you* – what you're feeling.

2 Now step into your chosen fantasy.

3 Take a look around: see the scene, the other person or people inhabiting it.

4 Let the eroticism you've already experienced in your solo sessions suffuse you again.

5 Let go to the pleasure and flow with it, and the fantasy.

6 As the sensations deepen to a very real physical level, 'give' the arousal you're experiencing to your partner – allow his or her touch and movement and your physical and emotional connection to take over and lead your mounting enjoyment. Let your partner take responsibility for stimulating you and flow with the pleasure he or she is giving you.

7 If you start losing impetus, go back to the fantasy and once you're back in flow again practise giving your real-life partner the ability to turn you on, drive you crazy and, finally, push you over the brink into orgasm.

8 Enjoy the feeling of closeness and tenderness for each other as you both come down from the high of orgasm and luxuriate in the delicious soft aftermath of contentment and satisfaction.

Finding your fantasies

Appreciating the whole scope of your imagination, your ability to let go and experience pleasure, your capacity to enjoy all your senses to the full – all this lies at the heart of your sexuality, the core of your being and self-esteem.

If you've ever said, 'I've no imagination' or 'I can't read fiction' or 'I'm not creative' then, somewhere along the line as you grew up, your teachers have drummed your senses and creativity into this belief. Lose it now – let it go for ever – for it is false.

The truth is that you – body mind and soul – have the most glorious, powerful vision and energy. You can fly, dance, paint, love and live life to the full. There is nothing whatsoever to stop you from being *you*– the best, most original, wonderful *you*. You are a shining star, a source of light and love and hope and joy for today and for the future.

The beauty of your imagination has no bounds, no walls, no locks. You are free to create beautiful pictures and stories and simply watch and enjoy, or walk within and live them for yourself. They will feed your creativity, your sense and enjoyment of self, and that will in turn feed and fire your sensuality and sexuality.

The more you complete your inner self this way, the more your everyday physical and mental self will flourish and this will in turn affect your sex drive and your ability to appreciate and support and enjoy your partner. Affection and love and passion will thrive from all this; as you and your emotional world strengthens and grows so will your ability to use your mind and your imagation. It's another circle and it's up to you, every step, every link of the way to say 'Yes' to it and go forwards. To live, and love, and be yourself – your true amazing self.

**The spiral
from fantasy
to fulfilment**

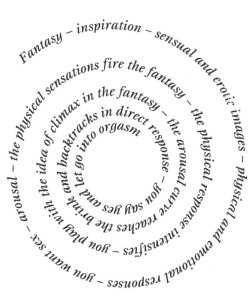

Sourcing fantasies

Fantasies are a highly individual choice. You want stories or scenes you conjure up easily, enjoy mind-watching or participating in, and respond to with a direct sexual turn-on or intensification. What's deeply erotic for one person might do nothing for you. You have to search for material until you happen on something that excites you sexually and rouses your senses.

Ideas to light up your mind and turn on your body

Books are a treasure store of erotic suggestions, ideas and explicit scenes. Read where your heart and taste take you but focus on the books where it's clear the author understands about eroticism.

Romantic novels do it for some – or your might prefer thrillers that stray into sex where the pace and tension of the plot heightens the excitement of the passion. Or the literary genre, maybe, where the sex may or may not be graphic but the depth of feeling and intensity of writing empower the eroticism.

Read to broaden your mind and your sexuality. Books are your heritage and provide instant access to a fantasy world and another dimension of being.

But in the meantime, or to save you time initially, I recommend an anthology of fantasies or erotic passages to photocopy in your mind. See page 175.

One way to get into a fantasy is to focus on erotic scenes and imagine how you'd produce them if you were making the script into a film. See the colours, feel the scents, tastes, touch of the lovers, watch the film in your mind and let it work its magic on your body.

Movies and television dramas are good hunting ground for fantasy inspiration too. Remember the scenes that turn you on and watch them again, or play the lead, when you're anticipating or having sex.

It doesn't have to be a whole story or even scene. Your fantasy could be one simple action that you find exquisitely sexy. One man I spoke to said he only had to imagine himself stroking his fantasy woman at the back of her neck where stray tendrils fell from her loosely coiled-up hair. 'The beauty, softness and overwhelming impression of her femaleness makes me feel very tender, and very aroused. It's all it takes.' Others weave detailed story lines and complex dialogue and action sequences. How you want to fantasize is all in *your* mind.

Recognizing the Fantasies That Turn You On

You won't find the awareness, the buzz of excitement, the turn-on, when you don't know what you're looking for. But the feeling will find you and it's unmistakable – you'll know it immediately. You'll live the book if you connect with its sensual message, you'll feel like dancing in the moonlight when you come away from a deeply erotic film and, most of all, you'll feel vibrantly sexy. All you have to do later, to recall the feeling and translate it into real life, is to re-live it as fantasy, in your mind. Your body will do the rest.

What about pornographic films and magazines?

Listen to your gut feeling. Anything that doesn't have the feel-right factor for you is out.

You want great sex. You want to luxuriate in your sexuality. Anything you feel bad about or which your mind or your gut or your body tells you isn't right for you is going to detract from your quest for sexual wholeness.

I can't tell you where you draw the line – everyone must

make their own boundary and yours could vary a lot even from your partner's. That's why sensitivity to each other's choice of fantasy and respect for each other's privacy is important. These are my guidelines:

♥ If a fantasy gives you the creeps or feels seedy or distasteful, press the cancel button in your mind and introduce another one. You may have to keep saying no to fantasies for a while, but your mind will soon learn what feels right for you. Then you'll come up with ideas that suit you much better so you can choose one that makes for great sex with no unease to spoil it.

♥ Remember you are in control of your mind and your fantasy world. Make it a welcoming place you're glad to visit: rapturously sensuous, exciting or daring, exotic or avant-garde. You'll come away feeling fantastic – enhanced by the wonder of great sex.

FANTASY AND LETTING GO

When a fantasy triggers arousal it's not subtle – it's dramatic, electric and unmistakably sexy. It's like letting go of inhibitions – your mind drops you down a level into a state of readiness for and welcoming of sex. You feel it immediately in your body. And the more you fantasize, the more easily you'll be able to relax into pleasure and arousal at will – either on your own or when you're having sex.

Sexy dreams and how to harness their eroticism

When you awake out of a sexy dream don't just think 'mmm that was lovely' – hold the dream while you think quickly through it and memorize all the images that come to you.

💜 How did it feel?

💜 What colours do you remember?

💜 What were the sounds, tastes, scents?

💜 How did your lover's or your touch feel?

Feel through your answers and re-experience the dream and most of all the eroticism, arousal and easy ability to slip into the sweetest climax. Stored in your sexual memory you can bring back the dream in all its intensity as a fantasy.

Encourage sensual, spicy dreams by saying to yourself just before you drift into sleep: 'Dreams of beauty and love and mind-blowing sex please.'

Sweet dreams will be yours.

Treasure your fantasies and use them to uplift your spirits and your sex life.

The Third Secret:
The Impact of Touch

♥ ♥ ♥ ♥ ♥ ♥ ♥ ♥ ♥ ♥ ♥ ♥ ♥ ♥♥ ♥ ♥ ♥ ♥ ♥ ♥ ♥ ♥

Touch can be mind-blowingly sexy. With the right person, the right mutual mindset, it can send you to heaven. In the whole depth and breadth of sexuality, at many levels and layers of meaning, the power of touch is profound. So explore and glory in the ability and power of your touch and your partner's. Touch is about connection – mind, body and soul connection. And the connection can transform your enjoyment of sex and light up your relationship.

Affectionate touch feels hugely meaningful – and it is. It evokes your earliest responses to affection as it was your first, pre-verbal experience of love, tenderness and nurturing. Your mother cuddled you, held you close, caressed you. And now, when you're lovingly touched, feelings and memories flood in of that time before words when touch meant so much.

These messages of affectionate touch, passed from parent to child all down through the ages, transfuse your relationship with trust and a feeling you're safe and cared for. The power of touch is primeval – mothers and babies, children, adults right through to the oldest ages, lovers – all bask and flourish in the contentment of touch.

Soothing caresses soothe the heartbeat of both stroker and stroked. Your body also reacts by soaking you with feel-good hormones. Emotionally you relax and respond into a positive frame of mind, stress drifting away. So even when the touch is apparently non-sexual, it helps keep your attitude to sensual touch positive and flexible. Be tactile: cuddle, hug, hold each other.

Connect with the Electricity of Touch

Touch is a potent energizer of arousal in your relationship. It can spark or signal desire, pulsing and controlling the speed of arousal. When you want your partner very, very much – like at the beginning of an infatuation or full-blown love affair – touch is automatically electric.

All you want to do is get close and feel their body next to yours. You can't keep your hands off each other – or would much rather not have to. Any opportunity and there you go – caressing each other, holding hands, arms around one another. You maybe stroke or tickle each other – for hours on end – pleasure-giving often purely for the giving and accepting of pleasure and affection. Because however sensually pleasurable, touch doesn't necessarily lead to sex.

And it can always be like that throughout the longest of relationships, if you let the feelings surge through you again, emotionally as well as physically brilliant. For touch can feel as exotic and be as potent as ever, at any stage of a relationship, drowning you with good emotions, and fun into the bargain – a triple-faceted bonus of joy.

Touch retains its power long after the initial in-love phase and can influence it right the way through. Don't miss out – use the potential and never neglect the pleasure and language of touch. For in the physical, sexual and emotional stakes touch can be a great leader or go-between. It's a channel for togetherness in all sorts of ways and gives a rich, rewarding edge to sex.

FIVE TOUCH TIPS FOR A TACTILE RELATIONSHIP

♥ Touch often – the more you do it, the more natural and relaxed it feels.

♥ Vary your touch – places, pressure, pulse and pace.

♥ But note your partner's favourite experience of touch and do it that way often.

♥ Show each other how you'd like to be touched – you won't always be psychic!

♥ Touch lots in public – openly as long as it won't offend anyone, and discreetly where it would. Touch draws you close.

Touch – the great communicator

Simple yet sophisticated, intimate and direct, touch beats every modern medium of technology outright in the world of emotional communication. Bypassing words, the physical sensation makes an instant connection with emotional and sexual links.

The language of touch

On a practical level it's useful, as well as schmoozily close and personal, to develop a language of touch with your partner – your own special soundless language. Understanding this secret and unique code is intimate, sexy and as close as the touch itself. Be alert to possible different meanings. Use your touch to communicate all sorts of messages as well as simple expressions of love or desire. Pay attention to touch – yours and theirs – soak it in.

Something as simple as the touch of your hand on theirs can transmit all sorts of messages in confidence: it might be a warning to listen carefully, or be cautious in what you're saying, a reminder of something that needs to be done or said, reassurance that all is well. Your touch can also express condolence, empathy, inspiration and solidarity. All with the intrinsic sexiness of intimacy.

SENDING MESSAGES WITH TOUCH

Enjoy sending messages of touch that are explicitly sexy. Start with these classics and go on to invent your own relationship language:

 Wherever your hand is resting on them, three gentle presses mean I love you.

 You're holding hands. Circle a caress with a couple of fingers in their palm to communicate 'I want you.'

 Rhythmically press with a fingertip wherever your hand happens to be resting on their body to remind them of the last time you had sex.

It's intimate, it's sexy, to speak the same language of touch that no one else hears or understands.

Affection

Except in the most casual of sexual encounters, affectionate touch is as vital as sensual arousal. When you really like your partner and show it with touch it breeds warmth and a feeling of closeness in the moment, however your relationship is panning out.

Even when sex is far from your minds, it's great to be tactile and close. Always take time to enjoy affectionate touch for itself and the emotional bond it will create between you. No matter if sex is off the agenda – keep in touch anyway. The emotional and physical closeness of loving touch will nourish your sexuality and the sexual bond between you even if it's currently sleeping.

If your partner's a woman:

Touch is particularly important to women because girls are usually brought up with a stronger emotional bias. Through older childhood years and into the teens, girls are more likely to still be cuddled and caressed to reassure them when things go wrong. All through women's lives, touch continues to mean a lot.

So be very tactile with your partner. Stroke her, cuddle her, sit or lie close to her, hold her to you. She'll see you as her protector, her confidant, and her friend, and each will strengthen her attraction to you as her lover.

If your partner's a man:

Touch doesn't figure so much in boys' lives once they're past the toddler stage, so it has huge impact when they're adult. Men love to be held. It helps heal the hurt of their parents' apparent withdrawal when they were encouraged to be more grown up and less emotional and vulnerable than they were ready or needed to be.

So it can create a terrific bond between you and your partner when you hold him close and safe and comfortingly.

In satisfying the need that was once denied, you enable him to become complete. It helps him feel confident and strong.

Hold him close – it will mean a lot to him and so will you.

Touch, attraction and invitation

Most people are insecure, scared of being thought pushy, anxious you might think they're coming on too soon, too fast or too clumsily. Touch can bypass all of that and give partners or prospective partners the sign they need that it's OK, you do want them, they haven't imagined it, you're every bit as attracted as they are. If you suspect this is what's going on with someone you fancy who's not meeting you halfway, or with a partner who's not coming across sexually, use touch to give them the message that yes, you want them.

You could of course say or do something else to attract or invite them, but then there's no going back – it's out in the open and, if they don't want to know just now, it will feel more of a rejection. Touch can be so subtle that if it isn't picked up the invitation will dissolve so subtly your ego won't suffer – it could have been a gesture purely of friendship after all.

So go on – if you want to show someone you already have a rapport with that you want them, reach out and touch them. If the magic is mutual, your gentle caress will lift it into life.

Fire desire

Tantalizing touch, the sort that builds desire steadily to the point of no return and beyond into climax, is sure, not tentative, firm but sensitive. It might, early on, be meant to tease, and then let you both idle blissfully in sensation, before moving on, exciting, encouraging, leading the way through the path of arousal, driving, coaxing, yielding, giving and taking.

Make your sexual touch magic

1 Think slow but sure.

2 Think of your partner's pleasure. Touch them as you'd like to be touched, but sense, from their touch, their individual preference and try their way too.

3 Respond (see below for tips on tact and sensitivity) and encourage them to approve or guide you differently if necessary.

4 Take turns in giving and receiving pleasure. Sometimes you just can't appreciate personal pleasure when you're concentrating on what you're doing to them. So you need to focus, every now and then, on what's going on in your body.

5 Be generous with your approval when it's good, getting better and reaching 'Yes!' level.

6 Don't lose contact if you get there first – well OK, you can't really help it in the oblivion of ecstasy, but only for those few moments. Keep in touch even if it's just to hold them close for a little while. Then focus on them and let your happiness intensify theirs.

Secrets Of Great Sexual Touch

If your partner's a woman:

A woman's body – just about all of it – is an erogenous zone. Your partner wants lots of touch, lots of pleasuring: sensitive but sure, slow but positive, all over, but especially the places special to her. So find them out.

These are some of the best:

♥ Her neck: either side of the spine and around the hair line at the nape

- Her face: the chin line, temples and forehead
- Her ears may be especially sensitive too
- Her back and shoulders
- Her ankles and feet

Practise different touches to find out what she likes: stroking, pressing, very gentle scratching or rather raking with your nails or, if that's too ticklish, your fingertips. Your touch can relax her, or empower her natural arousal responses. Use the power of your touch, not just for her pleasure but for yours too. Not a moment will be wasted: mutually mind-blowingly good sex takes time so every second you put in will add intensity, right the way through, for both of you. Don't begrudge her an instant – you'll only lose out yourself. Giving pleasure is as good in its own way as receiving.

Hold back on focused sexual touch until she's clearly becoming sexually aroused – be very sensitive to her eagerness. Remember, she is an individual and her responses won't necessarily be the same as your former lovers'. Discover what she likes – aim to be her best lover ever. Read books, watch videos if you'd like ideas and help (see page 175). But here are some ideas:

- Let your touch be firm and sure but gentle too. Some women complain that their partners are too rough and may even hurt rather than pleasure them. Her nipples and her clitoris are very, very sensitive – always respect that and avoid hurting her. Only deepen the pressure of your touch if she specifically asks or indicates you to.
- Feel or gently pulse her clitoris with your fingertips, don't rub. Ask her whether she likes it to be touched directly, or prefers just above, through the hood of skin covering it, or up a bit further towards her pubic bone, or to either side. All this can be amazingly sexually sensitive for the clitoris is

far more than is outwardly noticeable. The outer lips of her vulva and the pubic bone area are all clitorally sensitive and a gently pressing, pulsing, stroking touch, with your fingers or mouth, will probably build her arousal faster and more certainly than anything else.

♥ Remember that after all sex, except the occasional quickie, most women like the intimacy and affection of ongoing contact. It doesn't have to be pro-active touch – probably she wants to lie still and enjoy the feel-in-heaven endorphins and dopamines that engulf her after good sex as much as you. But do lie close together in each other's arms or snuggling against each other. Neglect this at the relationship's peril – it's vitally important.

If your partner's a man:

Again, every man is different, so take time to find out what your partner likes. All of it, he'll probably say, but persevere. Encourage him to be aware of his responses and tell you about them while you're having sex or later so that you know how best to pleasure him with the touch of your hands and mouth.

Learn about technique – see the list of books on page 175. As a starting point here are some ideas:

♥ Most men like to be explicitly sexually touched almost straight away and that's fine – but, until you're both ready to get on the last-stage fast-track to climax, encourage his whole body sensuality and sensitivity to match yours. Try all the forms of touch suggested in the 'if your partner's a woman' section and ask him which he likes and which especially turn him on.

♥ If he moves your hand away from an area, or says or shows he'd prefer a different way of touching, remember so you can concentrate on his favourites in future and avoid anything he's not keen on. Stroke his chest and see if he likes his nipples caressed by your hand or mouth. Smooth his calves, thighs – anywhere and everywhere. Memorize a map of him in your mind, marking all his erogenous zones and also any no-go areas.

♥ Use a firm, but never gripping, touch on his penis. Tentativeness frustrates – a sure, definite holding turns on.

♥ Use lots of lubricant; your own saliva's fine if you're alternating oral and hand stimulation. If you're sticking to hand touch, keep some lubricant close by and top up if ever your hand is rubbing rather than gliding.

♥ Keep the movement of your hands steady. Don't rub – wrap your hand round his penis and move the foreskin if he has one, over the shaft, slowly up and down. Forget all about any kind of frantic 'wanking' movement – think sensuality, think sex. This is about deep, deep pleasure and you're building his intensity slowly, surely and sensuously. Don't rush it.

♥ Find his orgasmically good places – the line that runs right down the underside of his penis, the frenulum (where the foreskin joins the shaft), and his G spot, where the two meet.

After you've both climaxed, encourage him to stay close, as you both come back down to earth, by being peaceful and still. Men have sometimes got into the habit of being hyperactive after climax, not sexually but wanting to get on with their day-to-day life. Maybe this harks back to caveman days when men were vulnerable to predators while having sex, so they made it as quick a process as possible. Men today (or at least most) are relaxed about enjoying prolonged sex, but their natural or learned inclination can still be to get up, washed, dressed and away immediately they've come.

So if your man is raring to get up and away after sex, help him learn a different and much more satisfying (for him as well as you) way. Hold him, shush him gently, show him through your touch you want him to stay close for a while longer. If he's satiated he may be worried you'll want more. Let your contented calmness show him all you want is to luxuriate in the intimacy.

Alternatively he may be the type who succumbs completely to the feel-good hormones of climax and wants only to sleep. Indicate through touch that's fine – but in your arms please, or like spoons, so that you keep the feeling of closeness while he slips into sleep. That way you won't feel abandoned.

A WORD ABOUT KISSING

I've been assuming that your sexual touch will be with your mouth as well as your hands. But all through sex, do keep coming back to mouth-to-mouth kissing – it's tender, and very, very sexy; it's also the ultimate intimacy. Kissing, an art in itself, is an intrinsic part of great sex. Show your partner, with your kisses, what you like. And 'listen' to what they're telling you about their desires with their kisses. Generally remember:

♥ Not too wet – think silky, not drippy

♥ Tongues positive but yielding – not hard and pokey

♥ Lips sensitive too – think sensual and warm

Touching and teaching the way to great sex

We're at least as sensitive when we're having sex as when we're thinking about it. More so, probably, for now more is at stake – the pleasure of the moment, the climax of joy, and all the emotional innuendos and consequences. So in sex, more than any other subject or activity, the greatest sensitivity is crucial. And it's where touch soars in importance for touch is a gentler guide than even the softest sound or word, and less liable to misinterpretation than facial expression.

Touch shows, illuminates, guides ...

It leads your partner easily, maybe unconsciously, or perhaps in enjoyable awareness, to wisdom about you and your unique sexuality. There's no loss of face, no suggestion (implied or taken) that they're not so hot in bed, no shame or blame whatsoever on either side. Just 'this is how I am, this is how I like it, this is how I like you and what you do', in easily absorbed messages of touch.

1 Hold your partner's body with your hands, using them to ease away or pull towards you their closeness.

2 Gauge their receptiveness to your message and increase or decrease the firmness of your touch. They may respond to the lightest pressure if they're used to 'listening' to touch, or need a firmer indication of what it is you're 'saying'.

3 If you like where your partner's touching, but want them to adjust the intensity or speed, show them by guiding their hands with yours. Or, if they're sensitive, show them the way you want to be touched with your touch on their body.

4 If you don't like your partner's touch – it hasn't hit the best places, or just isn't doing anything for you there today – then again, guide them with your touch. Take their hand or more specifically if necessary, fingers, and move them gently but positively to the right place for you now.

Massage – The Ultimate Luxury of Touch

Massage – oh it's so good. It can be the fore-runner of great sex or a sensual heaven in its own right. You don't know? You've not experienced the bliss? Then you have the most amazing pleasure in store! Read on, teach yourself and your partner the art of massage, or pay for a professional masseur to show you the how, what and why of sensual massage.

It isn't just the physical element – massage is emotionally therapeutic too. It's much like counselling in that it's so incredibly warming and good to have the whole, devoted, focused attention of another person for a relaxable, recognizably long period.

And it's amazingly, deeply sexy. Don't be alarmed – if you are massaging a friend purely as a friend, there need be no sexual vibes between you. Where the relationship between you is platonic, the effect on your sexuality will be contained within the completeness, the oneness of you alone and won't connect you. But your body and soul will positively hum with sexual energy after your massage, not the turned-on sort, but the most amazing whole-person, full-of-vitality, life-charged feeling.

Massage with your partner can be real, hands-on, super-charged sex, no holds barred if you both wish. But again, if you offer or accept a non-sexual massage, it doesn't have to be sexually arousing. Yes, it will give you the aftermath feeling of basking in your glowing sexuality just the same as the platonic variety above, but it doesn't have to lead to sex if one or both of you would rather it didn't. If you don't want sensual massage to turn to sexual massage, though, do establish this before you start, and stick to it to avoid potential problems of differing expectations in the future.

Massage with your partner is loving – you wouldn't devote half an hour or longer of your time to each other's pure undiluted pleasure if not. And although massage can be amazingly emotionally and physically and sexually healing the main purpose is pure, concentrated mind-blowing pleasure. It's animal, earthy and delicious, wonderful in itself and a sensational adjunct to great sex too.

GROUND RULES OF MASSAGE

❤ Your mutual agreement.

❤ You always take turns. Half an hour (or whatever time you choose) for you, half an hour for them at a chosen later date or vice versa. However generous or mean you both are you have to do this on a fairshares basis or it will breed resentment eventually.

❤ You must have a warm setting. Massage just doesn't work if one of you is cold.

❤ Unless you're both experienced at massage and trust each other implicitly to give it enough time, set a timer (or more subtly let the CD you play gauge the time) – this gives the masseur the stamina to keep going and the one being massaged the relaxing confidence of knowing it isn't suddenly going to stop short.

❤ The one being massaged chooses the music but it must be something with a soothing tempo and beat. Something they love which will add to the pleasure (more on this in Chapter 9).

❤ The masseur chooses the oils – more on this in Chapter 8.

❤ The one being massaged can choose to be, or not to be, massaged in certain areas. For instance, you might love your shoulders, neck and back being massaged and ask your partner to concentrate the massage there. Or you might say, 'Please don't touch my tummy.' The wish of the massaged is the masseur's command. This is important because if the masseur doesn't listen or ignores requests, the massage will lose its power to please and cause bad feeling – not the point at all.

Similarly tune your massage technique to your partner's preferences. Start by massaging as you would like to be massaged, but ask for feedback. Say 'Is this firm enough?' or 'Would you like me to do this differently?' If they're not happy and you can't seem to find the touch they want, ask them to show you on your back (or wherever) the way they'd like to be massaged.

MOST PEOPLE LIKE MASSAGE THIS WAY:

Slow movements

A firm touch

A kind of kneading action – either with your fingertips or the heel of your hands

Thumb pressing – this is great for tension spots. Get those thumbs in where you feel knotting; ask your partner to guide you there if necessary

Sensitivity to their response: if they murmur 'oh that's wonderful' don't move on, concentrate on that place a while longer and try deepening the pressure, particularly when thumbing tension spots

Top up with oil often so that your hands glide easily over their skin

❦ If they fall asleep that's fine, but make sure their head is comfortable. If you think they'll get a stiff neck wake them very, very gently after a few minutes.

❦ Think healing, not therapy. Remember that your hands are massaging to give pleasure to the skin and soothe tired or stressed muscles. Don't ever manipulate or put pressure on bones, particularly the spine, or nerves. If in doubt, go gently – your partner can ask you to deepen the massage if your touch is too light.

Mostly – enjoy, no matter whose turn it is to massage or be massaged; both are pleasurable in their own right. So when you are the masseur, take pleasure and pride in developing and using your skill. Good massage is a gift for both of you.

Touch is for you and your partner – however, whenever and wherever you both want – drawing you close, connecting and keeping you in warm contact. Reach out to each other and enjoy.

The Fourth Secret:
Scents and Sensuality, Appetites and Feasts

♥ ♥ ♥ ♥ ♥ ♥ ♥ ♥ ♥ ♥ ♥ ♥ ♥♥ ♥ ♥ ♥ ♥ ♥ ♥ ♥ ♥ ♥

Food and feasts and scents and sensuality: they entwine and link and celebrate life, dancing together in a zest for sex and love.

So free yourself to choose and savour delicious, life-giving food and abandon yourself to the sinking, soaring gloriousness of great sex and/or true contentment in your sexuality. Let go of inhibitions and explore and enjoy the good food/good sex connection. Be alertly alive to the sensuousness of these vibrant appetites. Embrace the emotional potential too: look after yourself and your partner by eating and loving well. No one else can do it for you – you owe it to yourselves.

It's sexy to be passionate about food
Develop a passion for food – it's fundamentally sexy. People who adore everything about food – preparing it, feeding others, eating and maybe growing it too – are usually people with an empathy for life's pleasures and positivities, including

good sex and a healthy sexual self-regard. It's as natural to savour the look, taste and the eating of food as it is to revel in the sensations of sexual being and appetite. And there's the same joy to be had in appreciating and satisfying our individual and shared senses and hungers.

Psychologists point out it's the oral gratification link between eating and sex that's erotic. Sure, sharing food and love and sensual bodily pleasure is all mixed up in our minds just like touch is; ever since, as babies, we're cuddled and held by a loving mother to the breast or bottle. But the linked eroticism of food and sex is far more than that.

Great sex and good food are two of life's hugest pleasures; delight in one encourages appreciation of the other. And not just physically, there's a spiritual dimension at work here too. For in celebrating these natural gifts of life you're praising and giving thanks for your creation. And in feeding others thoughtfully and carefully, and in sharing sexual joy with your partner, you touch into another dimension – love – which is, after all, what life is all about.

Forsake fashion – think curves

Don't let your natural sensuality around food be sabotaged by the current fashion for undernourished, fatless bodies. Let's tell the truth: thin isn't especially sexy. Flesh feels great in bed and so does a passion for life.

Let's all turn fashion on its head and be honest. We're fed up with feeling we should emulate skinny people. We believe in life and love and that means believing in food and your perfectly natural right to eat well and enjoyably.

Celebrate your life and your sexuality by celebrating the gift of food. If you take an interest in food values, and love yourself heartily, you'll naturally eat healthily as well as lustily. No need for diets: eat your way to feel-good fitness with respect and love for your body and you'll naturally find the weight that's right for you.

So lose your eating and sexual inhibitions and self-consciousness and be a gourmet for food and sex. You have all that pleasure to gain and nothing to lose.

Feed yourselves lovingly and let the love spill over into sex

Eating, together, the food you've lovingly prepared lifts your rapport and you feel good emotionally as well as physically.

One of the reasons has roots way back down the ages again, this time to campfire and cave community eras when eating together meant eating better and more safely. It's great for families too. What eating together gives to you and your partner is a time to relax, one to one, to talk and let each other in on your respective lives – the happenings, thoughts, hopes and fears. It's an intimate time; it affirms your importance to each other, your mutual respect and wish to understand and empathize and share pleasure. Is it surprising that it's sexy when all these points mirror the exact same components of good sex?

Think about the time aspect too. There's nothing whimsical about the idea of intimate, one-to-one meals together – they're great for relationships and they'll make your sex life sparkle too. So plan a little to make time to eat together – it's as important as making time to have sex together.

● ●

EAT SENSUALLY

♥ However simple or complicated the food, let the ingredients be good quality. It shows you care about yourself and your partner.

❦ Choose organic, free-range foods – it shows you care about other creatures and your environment, which indicates sensitivity.

❦ Present the food attractively. Bread and cheese can look wonderful, if served in beautiful baskets, wooden platters, china with a prettily set table and fresh flowers. You eat with the eye is a famous and very true saying. Again, it shows care for yourself and others and it's creative.

❦ Be adventurous often, or at least sometimes. Try new foods, new recipes. It makes you feel good to be doing something different, the new tastes will give zest to all your sensual awareness.

❦ Prepare food that's openly seductive or aphrodisiac for evenings you want to be especially romantic and sexy.

Have fun – share an erotically charged feast

The best aphrodisiac of all is your mind. Think sex. Think about the things that turn you on, please you, build arousal, and drive you wild into orgasm. Reach the heights or just relax along the way in gentle bliss with any of your senses.

Eating a varied, healthy diet is the best nutritional aphrodisiac. Your sexual health is finely balanced with all the aspects of your general well-being and all need to be well fuelled or they could malfunction and upset the rest of the system.

ESSENTIALLY, FOR BRILLIANT SEX

(and this is good advice for everyday life anyway)

❦ Eat well. Good food will give you the nutrients you need for a high level of sexual energy.

♥ Eat food you love – choosing mostly from the healthy options but indulging in rich/sweet and even trash foods too if they'll give you pleasure. Just change the maxim to little and not too often! Treats will make you feel loved and relaxed and happy, and feeling loved+relaxed+happy = feeling sexy.

♥ Eat enough to know you've eaten generously, but not so much that you feel full and have such a fat tummy you feel frumpy. A good guide is to stop eating when you'd like another helping, but know you've really had enough.

♥ By all means have a glass or two of wine if you enjoy the scent and taste and let the whole sensual experience spill over into sexual awareness and sensuousness. But (sorry to be a wet blanket!) do remember alcohol dampens your reactions and too much of it will dampen sex as well.

♥ Gorgeous-looking food

♥ Delicious-tasting

♥ Easy to eat

♥ Light (I'm not being a spoil-sport – it's just that if you eat too much rich, heavy food your bodies will be so busy digesting they'll say no to sex)

✳ ✳

Love to cook and cook to love

Kindness and cooking show you care – both for yourself and those you're feeding. There's a certain sexy closeness about choosing and preparing food thoughtfully for your partner. They'll be touched you've gone to the trouble and, feeling loved, will automatically warm towards you. Feeding others is a heart-warming feeling, too. Encourage and welcome their appreciation, and be generous with yours too, when they cook for you. It's close, friendly and makes you feel good about yourself, life and your partner – and if you're thinking sex it will help make you both feel good about that too.

Make it all even better by taking the whole food bit into a spiritual dimension. Decide you're not going to feel stressed, hassled or pressured when you're food shopping or cooking, but relaxed and positive. You're doing this because you want to – for yourself because you deserve delicious food, and because you value your partner too. At the same time, keep in mind the enjoyment of eating the meal you're preparing. And embrace the idea, too, that good food = good health = vibrant sexuality. Eat to love and love to eat. Nightmare supermarket trips and rushed, impatient throwing-together of supper will be things of the past if you adopt this attitude. Instead of negativity, you'll enjoy assembling, preparing and cooking your food.

Food and spirituality and sexuality? Yes!

Help the sexiness of it all along even more by respecting the food you're preparing. This is fundamental to some of the world's greatest religions and it lifts the most mundane preparation tasks to a meaningful and creative level. Take in the colours and form of vegetables and salads; choose organically grown produce. It's worth paying a premium – you and your health are worth it. Think about the dry ingredients: where they come from, how you're going to season them.

If you eat meat, poultry and fish, choose it extremely carefully, making sure it had a good, cruelty-free life; find a supplier of free-range, and if possible organic meat and poultry. If sex and sexuality are holistically promoted by you, respect for other living creatures is essential to *your* self-respect. It's very, very important to your spiritual wholeness, which is important to holistically best sex and confident sexuality.

Some of the Eastern religions, which are also noted for their treasuring of sexual skill and enjoyment, make the awareness and appreciation of food preparation almost into an art form. You too can savour all the sensual aspects – taste, scent, look and texture – using them all to enrich your sensuality and, in the wholeness of things, your sexuality.

So do it – make time, make an effort to eat together, just as you take time to make love. The more you luxuriate in the love of feeding each other well, and enjoying, together, the sensations of hunger, taste and satisfying your appetites, the more your attraction and the greater your desire for and appreciation of great sex. You're worth it. Your relationship's worth it.

● ●

TASTE YOUR WAY TO SEXUAL VITALITY

Think food, self-love and health: think sex

Gorging mindlessly on food or sex doesn't make for great sensation or self-esteem. But with consideration you can heighten your sensibilities. Go up another level and you'll touch a new dimension altogether – practise revering appetite and taste, desire and sex, and you'll begin to understand these pleasures, even in their simplest forms, and the joy they can bring to you.

♥ Eat slowly.

♥ Put your knife and fork (or chopsticks or whatever) down between each mouthful. Concentrate on what you're eating rather than the next mouthful.

♥ Chew each mouthful well.

♥ Think about it. How does it taste? Savour the sensation.

♥ Taste the different foods on your plate individually. Compare them – be aware of each.

♥ Revel in the pleasure of the taste and the satisfaction as you eat.

♥ Tune in to any positive feelings beyond the immediate pleasure. Tastes can be emotive – you might remember how and where you ate similar meals with other loved ones, or with your present partner another romantic time.

♥ Express your enjoyment of the food and encourage your partner to as well. Share your enthusiasm and your pleasure; the bond you create will intensify the togetherness of sex, later.

Be a bon viveur

We all have to eat so why not delight in the joy of savouring the good food we're so fortunate to have? And just as you choose to give yourself sexual pleasure, or to have sex with your partner, you can choose to make it great and not just perfunctory, and to really enjoy the sensations rather than go through the motions for the sake of it.

Let your appetites for food and sex work in harmony to enhance each other.

Food to Super-charge Your Sexual Vitality – Emotionally and Physically

How you feed yourself has a direct and drastic effect on your health and that includes your sexual health. You want to be happy, and sexy and emotionally confident? Then pave the way by eating well. You want to look great? Eat well.

Here are some guidelines to get you going. Develop a keen interest in food values and learn more for yourself. It's fascinating, it's vital, it's common sense, but most of all it's fun. It feels good to look after yourself!

Sorry to start with a negative, but I promise it will have a very positive effect. Cut down on coffee, nicotine, alcohol and sugar. All upset metabolism and though they may make you feel better initially they just make matters worse by 'crashing' you later and upsetting sleep patterns and moods. Beware using too much alcohol as an aphrodisiac – it may make you feel sexy immediately but the effect is usually short-lived. Too much and when the fix fades you may disappoint your partner and yourself by craving sleep or finding yourself suddenly glum and not in the mood for sensuality and sexuality at all.

Do (but it's essential to check any dietary changes and additions with your doctor first) take the recommended daily amount (RDA) of the following supplements daily. They all have an important effect on our feel-good balance and should be taken in combination:

Vitamin B complex

Calcium

Magnesium, iodine, potassium and zinc
   (or multi-mineral capsule)

Halibut liver oil (Vitamins A & D)

Vitamin E capsule

Vitamin C

Do take the vitamins as I've indicated. Multi-vitamin pills usually contain too small amounts to be effective. However, we need such tiny amounts of the minerals that a multi-mineral supplement is sufficient. I suggest buying supplies of vitamins and minerals from a reputable, well-known chain of high-street chemists or a well-established health shop. Follow the recommended daily allowance. Don't be tempted to exceed it as certain vitamins and minerals have an adverse effect on health in larger doses.

Make sure your daily diet includes fruit, leafy green vegetables and/or salads and some natural (i.e. unsalted and unroasted) nuts and seeds. Whole carbohydrates too – like pulses, potatoes and wholemeal bread. Also, daily, some high protein food like eggs, fish, cheese, yoghurt, nuts, seeds and pulses. But go easy on meat and poultry as it takes ages to digest and can sap vitality in the process, so not more than once or twice a week. If you can buy organic foods they will save your body having to cope with the effects of chemicals used in production.

The Forgotten Aphrodisiac – Our Sense of Smell

Scent is one of the most potent senses in the sexual spectrum. Yet human beings have so desensitized themselves over the last few centuries, and with a vengeance in the last 50 years, with our obsession for not having the dreaded 'body odour', that we've all but lost it.

But not quite. You'll find you still pick up on overt scents consciously, and your subconscious is doing a great job on responding to the language of scent we've so assiduously tried to wipe from understanding.

When you fancy someone you've only just met it isn't only looks and character you're responding to, it's their hidden but very definite personal scent that's reaching out to you. Pheromones are the body's deliberately sexy magnet, but it's also your individual liking for an individual's body scents, and vice versa, that locks you into lust.

Washing, the friend of personal freshness, can also be the enemy of earthy desire. Scared that our sweat, or horror of horrors, our genital secretions, will be offensive, we wash and wash and wash.

Let's dissolve the myth. It's stale sweat and secretions that are offensive – the sort that lurks under the arms of tight sweaters, or in the crotch of your pants.

By all means freshen up after your night's sleep and the day's work and strenuous exercise sessions, and after making daytime love. But leave it at that. Your natural scents smell good to the unconscious mind of the attracted opposite sex and no one else will notice them, consciously or otherwise.

Sharing a scented secret

One couple who came to me for guidance found that their intimacy deepened when they discovered they shared the same inhibition and were glad to let it go. They both admitted to being scrupulously careful to get rid of any personal odour before they made love in case they offended each other. However, Sophie confessed to Daniel that the best aphrodisiac for her was to snuggle her face in his armpits and take deep breaths of the scent of his sweat as he became aroused.

'It's really sexy,' she told him. 'I love the soft, warm closeness to you and the smell. It's part of you and your desire for me. It turns me on like nothing else!'

Daniel was both surprised and moved by this; they'd just never talked about it before. Because he thought she was fastidious, he'd never liked to tell her that he would love to be able to enjoy her natural scents too. He found them a huge turn-on and not the slightest bit offensive. Freeing themselves to enjoy each other's scents accentuated their intimacy and their earthy reciprocation of each other's attraction and attractiveness.

So tune in to the perfectly healthy and very sexy smell of fresh sweat and secretions when you're making love. See if it turns you on. Let go and let it lead you on – it can make you feel wildly earthily sexy.

▷ **Use your sense of smell erotically.** Revel in the smell of your partner's perspiration; relax in the intimacy of the scent of their skin.

If your partner's away, take an unwashed shirt to bed with you for a sense of closeness to them. If you're travelling, send them letters, or a scrap of material, sprinkled with the scent you use. Triggering memories of each other like this will charge your desire for each other while you're apart and enhance the sex you share when you're back together.

Other scents to spark and build desire

Use the same scent: one you adore and are happy to be surrounded with. An easy way to wear scent is to dab it on your pulse spots (temples, wrists, behind the ears and knees and on the ankles) where the warmth will diffuse it, creating a sweet-smelling aura around you.

If you prefer to use spray don't spray it directly on to your skin but instead hold the spray towards you at arm's length and walk into the spray so that you're cloaked in the gentlest of mantles of fragrance. Fragrant soap, body lotion, pot pourri, candles, etc can all add to this source of sensory pleasure so associated with you and, for your lover, the sensual intimacy you share.

Men often love on their partner the traditional flower-based scents, especially those whose base oil is rose or lily of the valley. They're quintessentially feminine. They also like the spice vanilla and the more exotic florals like ylang ylang.

Women tend to like their lover to go for the woody, spicy scents, sharp or musky, like vetiver, especially with the floral undercurrent of lavender and jasmine.

Ask your partner what they like and wear a scent you both love. And encourage them to wear something mutually pleasurable too.

Perfume choice is so individual that you may need to sample lots of different scents before you discover any that you respond to with a big *Yes, that's wonderful! I love it!*

But a word of warning: don't ever try out any more than two scents at the same time. Sample one on each wrist; any more and you'll confuse your sense of smell and the arousal factor.

Hunting grounds for perfume testers include perfume counters and cosmetics counters (as most of the cosmetic houses have their own perfume ranges). For the natural floral and spice scents contact suppliers listed on page 177.

Bewitch your partner by mixing or switching
traditionally gender-oriented scents
Some of the most interesting and provocative scents are combinations of perfumes which were once thought to be specifically feminine or masculine. Mixing together these traditionally gender-oriented fragrances bemuses and beguiles.

Likewise, wearing a scent that you've previously found attractive on your partner or on another fanciable member of the opposite sex can make you feel amazingly sexy. Whether that's because you associate the scent with being turned on, or whether the wafted pheromones are working well is anyone's guess, but never mind – it works!

More and more perfume makers are realizing this and adding unisex scents to their ranges. And sales personnel on perfume counters are learning not to be surprised when a woman buys products targeted at men for herself, or vice versa.

Wake up Desire with Aromatherapy

First of all wake up to awareness of the powerful effect scent can have on your nervous system.

1 Find a simple, pure scent you love. There are some suggestions below, but it's imporant to choose one key essential oil, or blend a mixture, whose scent you both enjoy.

2 Sit quietly and cup a drop of the essence or the fragrant flower in your hands, and gently savour the scent.

3 As you breathe in, be aware of where you're sensing the pleasure. It won't just be in your nose; you'll sense the pleasure somewhere else in your body, perhaps up and down the sides of your neck and slightly back towards your spine.

4 Now put your nose against the source of the scent again and breathe in deeply, taking the perfume right down through you.

5 Sense, again, where you're feeling the pleasure from it. This time, or as you practise again later, you may feel it suffusing other parts of your body: further down your back, your upper arms, or like light flooding up through your head.

6 Relax. Revel in how good it is. Enjoy.

The dual benefit of aromatherapy

We can absorb the therapeutic elements of essential oils through our skin in aromatherapy massage and also, through our breathing, via an even quicker route: the soft inner tissues of the nose and throat.

Essential oils provoke an almost immediate response through the body and mind. They are thought to work through the hypothalamus in the brain to have a regulating effect on the endocrine system, encouraging hormonal balance.

Essential oils are often chosen for their calming or specific healing qualities. But there are also oils that stimulate – waking you up, inspiring you to creativity, or simply and directly turning you on sensually and sexually.

Choose your favourites from suggestions listed here, bearing in mind your current need: maybe you or your partner feels stressed and would benefit from an essential oil with relaxing qualities, or perhaps you feel you would like to liven up and should select a stimulating oil.

Warning: Whatever oils you choose, remember that all oils are potent and it's essential that you only use them diluted in a safe aromatherapy carrier oil (see below). If you suspect or know that you are are pregnant or unwell, don't use any essential oils until you have consulted a trained aromatherapist about their safety.

You can use a ready-blended oil (for suppliers see the resources section on page 177). However, it can be very satisfying to mix your own and to customize it to your own particular needs and preferences.

Basic recipe for an aromatherapy-massage blend of carrier and essential oils

♥ 48.5ml of carrier oil – for example sesame, sweet almond or sunflower oil

♥ 1.5ml of essential oil – that is a total of 1.5ml, whether you are using a single essential oil or a combination

Blend them together well by whisking in an open, preferably ceramic, container, or by shaking them up together in a stoppered bottle.

SUGGESTED ESSENTIAL OILS FOR SENSUALITY
Mind, Body and Soul

- Aphrodisiac: jasmine, ylang ylang, cinnamon, sandalwood

- Relaxing and balancing: geranium, rose, lavender, rosemary, petitgrain

- Uplifting and energizing: jasmine, neroli, bergamot

- Spiritual togetherness: frankincense, bergamot, myrrh

- Great for the skin: patchouli, frankincense, lavender

- Healing (body and soul): cinnamon, lavender, sandalwood

Follow the guide to massage in Chapter 7 or read more about massage, aromatherapy and recipes for sensual-oil blends in a specialist book (see resources on page 176).

During the massage, whether you are massaging or being massaged, take in all of the pleasures of aromatherapy: the bliss of the touch, the harmony of the scents, the appreciation of the personal attention, devotion and intimacy. And luxuriate in the way the sensuality of it all recharges your sexuality and zest for life and love.

The Fifth Secret:
Sound, Sex and the Rhythm of Life

♥ ♥

Sound connects you to the world around and allows you to relate to others. It's a form of communication and a source of pleasure emotionally, sensually and sexually.

Vibrate to the harmony of sound and sex and sensuality

It's said that everything on this earth has its own vibration: your body, other living and inanimate things, your soul, your sexual awareness, places, atmospheres and sounds. One of the easiest ways to tune your vibrations in to others is through sound. Listen for when sounds click with you – when you respond with pleasure to the sound or rhythm. Be very aware of your response and see if it links up with the vibration of your sexuality. Let's look at some specific sounds to give you the idea:

The magic of voice …

It's deeply, sweetly, sensuously sexy to thrill to your partner's voice. You know that feeling when you answer the phone and it's them and the pleasure of hearing their voice crackles all down your back? It's automatic to love each other's voices at the beginning of a relationship when you're fascinated with each other, but maybe the thrill's faded or forgotten now? Then re-awaken it – don't miss out on one of life's greatest pleasures.

TUNE IN TO THE LOVE OF YOUR PARTNER'S VOICE

❤ Listen to the sound.

❤ Take in the pitch, accent, tone.

❤ Think of the person and what their sound means to you.

❤ Register your pleasure at hearing them.

❤ Let it flood through your whole body.

❤ Feel it – enjoy.

Don't forget your own voice. Remember, it's an erogenous zone for your partner too. Be aware of how it changes when you're talking to him or her at different times of the day, how it deepens when you're thinking or talking of sex, how it softens when you're speaking lovingly, slows when you're being thoughtful, gets serious when you're responding to something he or she is worried about, excites when you're having sex, purrs when you're having satisfaction!

▶ *Use the power of your voices to help illuminate
your words.* When they're in tune, their sound can be a
language of emotional harmony and maybe love and they're
a potent force in sexual attraction too.

The magic of words and talking and listening ...

With everyone you meet, choose your words carefully: they
have the power to delight or give pain, to deepen
understanding or confuse. This is still important sexually if
you're single – consider what you say carefully. Aim to light up
other people's lives with your words, to be kind, or fun, or
sensitive, or supportive or helpful. Yes, you'll help others, but
you'll realize you're doing it for yourself too because it feels
great to be warm and positive.

It isn't cool to be frosty, or cruelly witty, or contemptuously
cutting. It might make you or others smile for a second but the
aftermath will, deep down and dangerously, be of sickening
self-dislike. Use your words carefully – like your actions
they will return to you. Think positive and you'll be automatically enhancing your whole confidence, including your
sexual confidence.

Same in a relationship ...

Stop and think when you're about to say something calculated
to bring your partner down. Stop and think if you're about to
launch into a tirade of negativity about your partner, or your
relationship – what you don't like, what's wrong. It will come
across as attack and either crush them or invite a reciprocal
barrage of hostility.

Think instead how you can express your feelings so that
they have a positive outcome for you, for your partner and
for the relationship. Anger, worries and other negative

emotions need to come out, but they needn't be destructive, they can be constructive and do things for you, good things, rather than destroy.

If rows or unpleasant tension have become a habit you can't seem to break or even to talk about, find a good relationship counsellor to mediate and help you re-route to a constructive, non-damaging way to sort things out. Or go on a basics of counselling course – it's fascinating and extremely helpful in learning how to manage see-saw or over-the-top emotions and transform fractious situations.

This is important sexually – for your own inner wholeness and sexuality and for your relationship. What you say and the way you say it can promote dislike, distrust and disillusion and, however temporary the effect is intended to be or will seem, the negativity will eat into its roots, the unkindness will poison them too, and the bond between you could wither.

POSITIVE TALK TO HEAL AND ENHANCE

Imagine, instead, that you're nourishing not just the relationship, but its foundations:

♥ Don't go in on the attack, impulsively or with forethought.

♥ Do use forethought to promote positivity.

♥ Think of your relationship and the love and/or attraction you share. Let its goodness influence what you're going to say.

♥ Use words as peace makers, bridge builders, translators, never as weapons.

♥ Use them to protect and enhance the inner, individual sexuality of both of you, not to harm it with verbal abuse.

♥ Use words to bring you together, not drive you apart.

How do your words sound?

Your voice and the things you say have an immediate and lingering effect on others and especially your partner. Listen to yourself occasionally – or re-run how you said things when you've a moment or two alone to reflect.

1 Do you keep your voice within a pleasant range of tone? That means not squeaking, or squawking or shouting or uttering any wince-making sounds – or at least, if you do, being aware of it and able to laugh at yourself and apologize to others.

2 Have you been negative, malicious, unsettling or critical?

3 How did others and especially your partner respond to you today when you spoke? Did they warm to you or back off – was your partner attracted by what you said and/or how you said it or were they repelled by your words?

4 How do you feel about what you've said today and the way you said it?

GOOD RESOLUTIONS

for your personal sound system which are in tune with the real you and your warm, outgoing, loving personality

♥ Speak low and gently.

♥ Speak clearly so you can be heard easily.

♥ Speak your truth from your heart.

♥ Speak with love and respect for the other.

♥ Speak to enhance the moment or the day for them.

Language and sex ... words and love

Through words, you can enter via sound and meaning an erotic dimension far more satisfying than erotic videos. For, in demanding that your creativity and imagination come into play, you simultaneously fire them with life.

Read erotic magazines by all means, and notice if it's not just the pictures that turn you on, but the words written around them and the articles.

In erotic scenes in movies it's partly the dialogue that sends shivers of your own sexual awareness and that exciting, wanting feeling through you, as well as the pictures. And to help you fantasize when self-pleasuring, an erotic story often fires your imagination faster than anything.

Words have immediate impact and stay in your head, for instant recall whenever they are summoned.

The words with most erotic potential of all are your own and your partner's. Use your own words to spark desire, arouse, excite and tip each other over the edge into orgasm. Experiment to find what kind of talk turns on your partner. Be clear in your responses to what they say, so that they know what you find erotic.

Experiment with sexual innuendoes and codes that you can use secretly in public, doubling their thrill and intimacy with intrigue. Build anticipation of sex throughout the day with suggestive talk – on the phone or in person. Think seductive, be seductive. And most of all use words to express your desire and pleasure and wanting when you're having sex.

Know when to talk, when to keep silent. You don't want to be self-conscious or irritating, you do want to feel, and be, sexy. Be natural – just express your feelings when you're both connected emotionally as well as physically. Other times let them concentrate on the sensations or their fantasy. When you do speak it will be more meaningful and have more impact.

If you're normally silent and you or your partner find it difficult to talk sexily, start with just a word or too – 'mm that's amazing'. It's always appreciated. Think to compliment – it will make you, and them, feel good. Accept compliments gracefully – if you rubbish them sooner or later they'll stop making them. If they say 'you're gorgeous' be glad and luxuriate in it – whether you disagree doesn't matter. They see you that way and that's wonderful – rejoice.

Think to be enthusiastic – you'll turn yourself on at the same time – positivity breeds positivity. Think to affirm they're doing great. Let them in on where you're at on the arousal curve. And let them in on your impending, and happening, orgasm. Be blissfully, wordfully appreciative afterwards – even if it's just the all-time-wonderful-to-hear-whispered 'Ohhh...!'

The promise of prose and poetry

Poetry is about beauty and truth and pleasure. It enhances best sex and the wholeness of sexuality so well because they share all these joys.

Do you like poetry and prose that strikes a chord with you? Do you find joy not just in reading it, but in sharing it with others – especially your partner? Do you respond to its beauty with feelings of your inner and vibrant sexuality or sheer, open eroticism?

If it's yes to all then you're already one of the poetry cognoscenti, which is great. But if not that's fantastic too because you've this whole new area of beauty to anticipate. Poems and books aren't daunting, or boring, or difficult (well, not usually and if you choose what you like at first and are open to expanding your horizons).

Reading's great fun and feels good and in particular, as far as your sexuality is concerned, it's a brightening of one facet of your sensuality which can enhance the whole.

You could start by browsing the poetry section in the library or bookstore – maybe with an anthology of love poems. When you find some that appeal directly, seek out more of the poet's work. Copy out sections you particularly like, memorize them maybe. Let them feed your own creativity. Think why they inspire you: the sound of the words, the meaning, the erotic sense they bring flooding through you?

And books. What's turned you on in the past? Re-read and seek out more of the passages where your sexuality reaches out in response. Not sure where to start looking? Then think of your favourite, sexiest films and borrow or buy the original book or maybe the screenplay and re-live it off the page.

Sharing sexually inspiring reading pleasure is intimate and erotic. So take it in turns to read to each other. You could be in bed, last thing at night. Even if you drift off to sleep lulled by your partner's voice, however much you love what he or she is reading, chances are the eroticism will fill your sleep and when you wake invite you both to share intoxicatingly sweet sex.

It doesn't have to be overtly sexy. Erotica is often surprisingly sensitive and subtle. So find your own favourite erotic moments in films or books. Watch or read them with your partner; if you're on the same wavelength they are likely to share your pleasure. In any case it will deepen their understanding of what turns you on. Get your partner to do the same.

Let the beauty and sexiness of others' words, whether the eroticism is by chance or deliberate, electrify your attraction to each other and spark arousal.

Timeless sex and sensuality in the classics

Go back to the classics for enduring eroticism and sexual verve and drive that still pulses today. Why do Shakespeare's plays still enthral on stage and screen, centuries after his life? Not just because he was hugely talented in the art of writing, not just because his stories were fascinating, the characters vivid – mostly because it's drenched in sensuality and eroticism and passion. Jane Austen's work is saturated with sex too – think of her title *Sense and Sensibility* – so cleverly ambiguous it got her past censorship in her day but which openly resonates with passion.

Then there's D H Lawrence and, in poetry, e e cummings, one of the first open-about-sex poets whose work is every bit as erotic and still stands as an inspiration to modern poets writing on sex and sensuality.

Modern literature is a wonderful source of erotic writing too and finding your own favourite authors and poets is fun. To start you off, try the latest anthologies (see page 175). Dip in and browse to see what turns you on or moves you. Make a note of the authors of your favourite books, order other titles by them and read on ...

HOW TO READ TO FIRE YOUR IMAGINATION AND SEXUALITY

♥ Read and read, as eclectically and catholically as possible so that you gather inspiration from many sources.

♥ As you read to yourself, hear the words in your head and let the sound turn you on as well as the meaning.

♥ Take turns reading your favourite romantically and/or sexually moving poems and passages to each other.

♥ Feel the inspiration of the words.

♥ Luxuriate in the closeness of reading to or listening to your partner.

♥ Draw close in intimacy .

♥ Have sex with the intensity and images and romance of the fiction, uplifting your thoughts and sensations.

Share each other's reading and sexual appreciation of poems and beautiful prose or dialogue. Fly on a sexual high with the spirit of the words. Literature is a part of your heritage – your sexual heritage.

Let Music Move You

Listen to music that moves you. Hauntingly beautiful melodies or amazing chord structures, rhythms and harmonies – whatever makes you want to sing or dance, whatever makes you tingle. Feel the waves of sensation that flood through you. Your circulation will be charged by a current of energy. Emotionally and spiritually, too, you'll feel inspired and uplifted. Music gives you a vibrant, moving sense of your sensual completeness.

The sexual harmony of melody and rhythm

1 As with your reading, have fun seeking out all your favourite music – the pieces and bands and singers and instruments and songs and operas – whatever appeals to you.

2 Take time to listen, really listen to the best bits, the sections that make you feel intense, empowered, inspired: that 'wow this is so amazing' feeling.

3 Then feel it, concentrate on sensation. Where it's affecting you in your body, how it's affecting your soul. Doesn't it make you want to sing, or move or laugh or cry or fly? Doesn't it make you long to have sex and add to the sensation with another, very physical and emotional one that lifts your pleasure to an even higher plane?

4 Practise tuning in on a regular basis to the magic of music and its effect on your sensuality and sexuality.

5 Let it lift you and carry you along. It could be the melody, or the poetry of a song's words, or the rhythm – or all of it.

6 Feel it and exalt.

Sex, poetry and rock 'n' roll

Some of our sexiest, most passionate, most emotional poetry can be found today in contemporary popular music. Home in on your favourite sexy lyrics, the ones that make you feel ultra feminine or masculine, the ones that make you feel wild and free and so good you could-do-anything-go-anywhere.

Choose the ten tracks that mean most to you; those that make you feel great, or move you with nostalgia or sadness. Think about why they make you emotional. Let the music, the lyrics, the feelings they awaken in you, enrich your life and your sense of sexual self. Feel the vibration of the music linking and buzzing with your own vibration – your aura, the energy field around you.

Moving to the music

And then draw your partner into the magic:

1 Listen to each other's favourite music.

2 Tell each other why the lyrics strike a chord, why you think they're so beautiful.

Then share the emotion. Music moves you, makes you feel emotional and so does attraction and love. Link the two. Use them together for increased awareness of each other's personalities, or the intensity or closeness between you. Use it for fun and laughter and to heighten or deepen the mood.

Dancing to ecstasy

Add another sensation by dancing – it's primitively, wildly sexual to let go all your inhibitions and abandon yourselves to the music you love. It could be real aerobic work-out type bopping to increase heart rate and release all the feel-good hormones that set the circles of arousal in motion. Or a slow smoochie closeness to generate the intense, electric build-up of wanting – your bodies resonating with the intoxicating eroticism and togetherness of dreams.

Dancing together, when you want each other very much and especially when you love each other, is sex.

Tune in to Stay in Key

Get to know what you both like – this is vital in a relationship. If one of you plays music the other dislikes, it's a huge turn-off because it's an insult, saying, 'I don't care about you, only myself and my pleasure.' Selfishness never made for good sex.

Find music you both adore and have fun seeking out new discoveries of musical harmony to soothe and enhance the bond between you.

Use music as an aphrodisiac

1 When you're having sex or thinking of it, play your mutually favourite things and let the sound stir your souls and bodies.

2 Pace yourselves to the music. Take your time, sometimes just holding each other and listening, other times moving gently together, other times beginning to build arousal more specifically.

3 Gradually let the music charge the atmosphere of desire and closeness between you. Feel the rhythm of the music pulsing and driving your sexual rhythm.

4 Double the pleasure of all the sensations by mixing the pleasures of sound and sex.

Choose music for health

Tune in to the music, literally, of life. Music in harmony with your soul – the music that lifts you and makes you feel not just alive, vibrant and sexy, but happy, and warm and in love with life and your partner.

You are constantly affected by sound. Make it, as much as possible, healthy, beneficial sound. Try to live where the background noises are ones you like. Avoid monotonous music whether in the background or chosen – it will make your life feel boring and gradually dull you down too.

♥ Look for beauty in the melody especially, so that your soul can sing along. Find a beat that's uplifting, not mesmerizing or fretful, and for lyrics that make you think and feel.

♥ Choose music that adds depth to your life and increases awareness of your happiness in sex and/or your sexuality.

♥ Make friends with your favourite music. Like a good friend, it will always be there to comfort or inspire or make you think.

♥ Use music to change your mood as you wish. To relax you when you're too stressed to feel sexy. To help you change to a higher gear if you're sleepy or lethargic and would prefer to feel sexy and up for it.

♥ Let music soothe ills and pains – it can be a potent force in healing (see Chapter 12) – and energize your whole sex system.

Music is magic. When you love music it lifts you and loves you. Music is sensuality in the medium of sound.

The spirituality of sound

The great composers and song-writers talk of a spirit of music and poetry working through them. Their creativity is a God-given gift, their talent for making beauty flows into sound.

When you listen to such music – be it Mozart or Brahms, Lennon and McCartney, Dave Brubeck or the latest pop/rock great such as Céline Dion or Robbie Williams – the joy of that talent flows on into you. At its best – when you're in tune with the beauty – it's a life-enhancing spiritual experience. You sense your one-ness with the power behind this amazing world you inhabit.

When the two of you, together, have this experience, it's another dimension again. Sublime. Delight in it and give thanks.

The Sixth Secret:
Tuning in to Your Sixth Sense

♥ ♥ ♥ ♥ ♥ ♥ ♥ ♥ ♥ ♥ ♥ ♥ ♥ ♥♥ ♥ ♥ ♥ ♥ ♥ ♥ ♥ ♥ ♥ ♥

All around you and suffusing you and others is an invisible energy. Your ability to sense it is potentially just as strong as your other senses. The more sophisticated our technical and scientific understanding, the more we've neglected the sixth sense that is still so fundamental to other animals' well-being. The more you learn to recognize and tune in to the various aspects of your sixth sense, the easier it becomes. It's well worth discovering: as well as being an increasingly useful and inspiring part of your life, it will add a richness to your sexuality and your relationship.

Tune in to yourself and others ...
The sixth sense is the way you sense when all is or isn't well with you, deep inside, and the way you can tune in to others' feelings too. It's the way you feel around others and especially

your partner. It's how you pick up on the atmosphere in a place. And extra-sensory perception has no boundaries or limits. You might, for example, sense a certain person is thinking of you just before they phone you, or you may even sense what they're thinking even though nothing's been said, nor outward sign given.

And to your partner ...

This extra sense also gives sensitivity in the way you're relating to each other and how the tapestry of your togetherness is being formed. Richly woven with fibres of character, strength and self-confidence, and mutual liking, respect and interest, all shot through with the shining thread of sexual rapport, the fabric of your relationship will be both beautiful and durable.

HOW TO TUNE IN TO YOUR INTUITION

Like most skills, the more you practise intuition the easier it becomes. Listening to your sixth sense means you can ponder the message and gently probe to see how you can use the information you've sensed.

♥ When a thought comes into your mind pay attention to it.

♥ Question whether it comes from your thought process or has arrived unasked, unorganized and unscheduled.

♥ If the latter, what is it telling you?

♥ How can you use it to improve your communication or understanding?

♥ Thank your mind for giving you the message and a way forward.

Sensing your sixth sense physically

Sometimes this energy can be experienced physically and you may have been aware of its texture, look, taste, or even scent. The more in touch with your senses you are, the more likely this is. You may also be particularly sensitive to it if you've managed to retain the simplicity and truth of childhood perception. The more you practise 'tuning in', the more you'll sense and recognize it.

* *

TUNING IN TO THE FEEL

Think of the finest tissue paper that light can shine through. Think silk, satin, velvet, taffeta, fine cotton or linen. Think sunshine rays streaming in and sparkling the dust in the air with silver. Think of breathing an atmosphere of clear, fresh, sweet-smelling mountain air that charges, and constantly recharges, your relationship. Think of floating or flying in a sweet-smelling, softest, cushioning, supportive bed of thistledown.

Think love – how would it feel if you could reach out and touch it? Perhaps you can?

* *

You know how you'll say of someone 'I feel at home with them'? Well, that's a sure sign your sixth senses are working in harmony.

Knowledge beyond words

When Rhian met her boyfriend Mark she had the strongest feeling he was her destiny. 'Our similarities draw us together, and even our differences are interesting and add zest, but it's more than that,' she explains. 'It's as though we're somehow "held" by our closeness. It's not claustrophobic at all but like

---

we're each running on our own tracks but parallel to each other at the same pace. Although it takes energy because we don't always get on well, we want to be there even if the going does get rough. And when everything's good it's like soaking up the warmth of pleasure. You know how sexy and sensual and great it feels to soak up the sun on a warm spring day when you feel you're at one with nature? That's the sexy, warm relaxation of the unspoken ambience between us. And it's always there, even if it sometimes goes into hiding!'

If you're happily tuned in to your sixth sense even though you're not necessarily aware of your own and others' auras, you'll be enjoying the advantages right now: warmth towards yourself and your sexuality and, if you're in a relationship, warmth towards each other, great liking, and good sex. If so, that's wonderful. But keep exploring your self and the relationship for it's always in progress. You're constantly growing and developing so keeping in touch with your sixth sense will allow your personal fulfilment and your relationship to flourish.

If, on the other hand, you know you're at odds with yourself or your partner, tune in to it with your sixth sense so that you can tackle what's wrong constructively. Think flexibly. Think openly. Allow yourself the luxury and freedom of admitting there might be a better way. Explore!

Using Your Sixth Sense to Oust Negativity

There is a rather confusing word for the current of negative emotional energy that can sometimes create a physical impression – glamour. It's not 'glamorous' at all as in our current use of the word, but unattractive instead. It comes from the same root meaning, though – the creating of an illusion. Perhaps because we tend to suppress the negative emotions like dissatisfaction and jealousy, when they do force their way out they do so in a swoosh of energy.

One of the most common glamours around is untruth, or dishonesty. Suppose you're in a relationship where you know you are denying your real feelings about your partner, to yourself and/or to him (or her). Or you sense your partner's discomfort with you, and either don't confront him at all, or accept his insincere protestation that all is well even though, deep down, you know it isn't. In letting either situation continue to exist, you've tacitly accepted the state of dishonesty – possibly completely but more probably subconsciously. Nevertheless it will cloud your happiness, dent your sexual confidence and dim the sex you share.

It's useful to get a physical impression of the dishonesty going on because it alerts you to problems you may not have noticed, or which you've misguidedly chosen to ignore. So let yourself sense it.

When you pick up on dishonesty physically you'll be most conscious of its texture. It's sticky, and resiliently clinging. It's like walking through a cobweb: it gets in your eyes and teeth and hair. You feel you want to shake it off but can't. If there's a high degree of sexual and emotional passion involved, it might feel like a cloying denseness that settles and layers through thinking and blocks your energy and dulls your desire. Some say it's like glue, making it difficult for you to move.

It snarls up sex because everything is a struggle, including sensual interaction, pleasure, and clear, constructive communication.

Using your sixth sense to help mend a relationship

When you don't know what's going on or why, it can help define it if you sense the physical traits of the ambience between you.

1 Step back for a second when you experience an emotion, and consider how it would feel.

2 Does it have a texture, or a scent, or an energy effect like warmth or a lightning strike.

3 How does it affect you? Good, bad or neutral?

4 Why do you think this is?

Or you could focus specifically on the sex you have:

1 Go into the room where you most often have sex and stand or sit quietly.

2 Be aware of the atmosphere there.

3 Ask how your rapport, or lack of it, is coming across to you.

4 Shut your eyes and wait for an impression. Remember it could come through to you in many ways. You could be aware of how it feels to the touch, or you might see in your mind's eye an image – a flower maybe or something less pleasant – or a particular colour. Or you might hear a sound, or detect a scent.

One man described his impression of the dishonesty between him and his partner as 'a kind of mental Velcro, holding me against a seam of untruth and constant unease in a rough, prickly, sludgy grip'.

A counselling client, not knowing how to leave a relationship she and her partner had pretended was far better than the sad reality, said it was 'like swimming in a muddy pool, thick and brown like treacle that stops me climbing out. It tastes sickeningly, poisonously sweet'.

But when the dynamics between you are good the physical atmosphere picked up by your mind will reflect it pleasurably. Describing their excellent relationship one couple said, 'It's like our emotions and sexuality are gliding effortlessly on skates over the smoothest surface – linked in brilliant harmony', and 'it's like savouring an unending supply of fine-quality wine and luxuriating in all its nuances with no fear of a hangover'.

Using the physical impact of the energy to improve your relationship and sex life

If you've not only become aware of dishonesty in your relationship, but are sensing how it's stifling your rapport and harmony, you'll understand how crucial your attention is. Negativity crowds the air you share and invidiously sickens the life you could be enjoying so much more vitally together. It's essential to open up, let truth in, and clear the fog that's at best spoiling things between you and at worst suffocating your relationship.

Great sex is an expression of intense attraction and high regard for each other. Don't let negativity spoil things.

The Row = Wild Sex Conundrum

Tension and distress release adrenaline and testosterone may surge in anger outbursts and in a basically sound relationship the energy often translates into arousal and great sex. It can be a splendid way to make up after a much needed frank exchange of views.

But when the relationship is in a terminal stage it's different. Divorced people often say, 'It's funny but when we finally admitted our marriage was on the rocks our sex life was suddenly revitalized.' But it isn't really great sex, it's driven, grieving sex: an expression of your terror and/or sorrow that all that is or could have been so fantastic between you is threatened or lost.

If you and your partner are at this stage, don't give up. If it's what you both want you can use all your senses to restore a true, close, alive relationship where great sex follows naturally and joyously. But if your relationship is OK although, like all couples, you're sometimes aware of difficulties or distance between you, face them now.

Clearing negativity

Your defensiveness may be so engrained you can't see the reasons for the negativity. Or perhaps you keep twisting them to give your partner, or yourself, the benefit of the doubt. Writing it all down can help. It's difficult to carry on pretence or a pantomime of denial or ignorance on paper. So pin it down:

1 Take a big sheet of paper and a pen.

2 Jot down all the points that are annoying or upsetting you about your partner at the moment.

3 Now imagine you're them and jot down the way they see it.

4 Get them to do the same.

5 Compare notes, but with interest and humour – no accusations or temper flare-ups allowed!

6 Take time to step into each other's shoes and see how it is to feel as they do.

7 Let the two-sided truth of the situation register. Memorize it for instant recall whenever either of you is getting pedantic or prejudiced in favour of self again.

An instant way to clear the debris and fog

1 Re-capture the physical impression of the glamour you've received. Think again of its texture or other qualities.

2 'See' its visual appearance. If you don't remember this imagine it as a pernicious mist hanging in the air around you like shrouds of cobweb.

3 Now, in your mind, take the nozzle on the hose of a vacuum cleaner, switch on the machine's motor and hold the nozzle in the air.

4 See the mists of dishonesty and negativity being sucked in. Move the hose and nozzle around to vacuum the whole room and/or the areas around you and your partner.

5 Visualize the air clearing as the last vestiges of dishonesty are sucked in.

6 See the light of new understanding, truth and wisdom flooding your relationship.

7 Feel the sense of release, peace and inspiration this gives you.

8 Now you can transform your relationship. Now you can begin to re-build happiness in yourselves and between each other.

Harmonize

In this new clarity and honesty – think sex, be sexy. The time may not be right to have sex; you will both know whether it is or not. But you are going to hold each other and tune in to the closeness you know is possible between you.

1 Both standing up, or lying stretched out, hold each other so that the length of your bodies are in contact.

2 Feel your partner's body against yours.

3 Feel your souls in contact too.

4 Shed any resurging feeling of resentment – in your mind shake it off as though you're shaking off water after a swim.

5 Feel the energy between you.

6 Kiss each other's necks and temples and noses and closed eyes.

7 Be aware of the tenderness.

8 Be aware of the sexual energy pulsing through you and between you.

9 Tell yourself, each of you, that you are partners, together and strong in your togetherness.

10 Be thankful, and glad. Take your time in this feeling.

11 Be together sexually: a long sensual kiss, touching each other intimately, making love, going on to have sex if you both want to.

12 Repeat this regularly. Once a day would be good. Never let more than two days pass without it. You want your relationship to be good, you want it to be wildly, deliciously sexual. This is an excellent way to start and keep the habit. Passion doesn't always just happen – you happen it.

You have great ability to grow and tend and bless your own inner sexual completeness and your relationship. Use your sixth sense in all its forms to replenish the energy of attraction and desire, arousal, orgasm and satisfaction.

Seamless sex

Great sex – to be ongoing – needs a firm foundation of rapport. Your mutual liking and the way you are around each other and the way you interact sets up and fuels an energy flow, an ambience, a meeting of your bodies and minds.

The energy pulses round all the 'rooms' of your relationship, funding an ebbing and running, but more or less constant awareness of each other. Sensitivity to each other's feelings instigates thoughtfulness and, coupled with care, you have kind behaviour. It's another circular self-fulfilling network. Feed it with positivity, common sense, ability and flair (all of which are yours to give – you only have to summon them to utilize them) and it will not only keep flowing but improve.

All the way round the circle there are connections which can cause bumps and blocks unless you circumvent them somehow – perhaps with an attention or attitude or behaviour shift, or a surge of extra energy or effort, and/or with talk or therapy.

All the time, for this flow to function, you're noticing each other's state of mind and body and your interaction. It's this awareness that lights up a relationship. With avoidance or disinterest of the other's state of being the relationship would be so dark and dismal it would slow it right down and maybe grind it to a halt anyway. But what helps massively in your awareness is if, instead of just noticing with your senses, you also intuit what's going on for them, for you and between you.

Empathy and sex

You'll send your own pleasure escalating and enable yourself to heighten your partner's too if you get to the heart of his or her experience. Empathy is an understanding so deep you live the feeling with the other person as though it's yours or at least as though you know how it is for them. It's as close to being at one as you can get, so trust – total, mutual, unreserved trust – is essential.

How to have the ultimate experience of sexual empathy …

During intercourse when your bodies are united the pleasure is mutual, close and intense:

1 Step back from the scene in your mind and, focusing on your partner's pleasure, imagine how they are feeling.

2 Feel what it's like to be them, around you.

3 Imagine how the sensations of your touch, the sound of you, the scent of you, are arousing them more and more as their arousal curves upwards towards orgasm, plateaus out and stabilizes until they reach the brink of orgasm.

4 Feel the intensity, feel how it is for them to let go and climax.

It may help if they talk you through it; either way you'll find it mind-blowingly exciting and if your heart's in it with them you may find your own arousal paces theirs and culminates in a resoundingly fantastic orgasm for yourself with or just after theirs.

Another time, help them empathize with your pleasure. Talk them through your feelings along your own arousal curve. Let them in on your own individual preferences: how you like them to vary the tempo, or pause completely maybe so that you can just concentrate on feeling their closeness and touch. Let them into your mind and heart: it's a deep, velvet, powerfully sweet, intoxicating intimacy. It will take the sexual pleasure and ecstasy you share into another dimension of pleasure, body and mind.

Make your home a sensual, sexy haven

Lastly some practical ways to create a welcoming and potentially erotic atmosphere in your home to complement your sexuality and all seven secrets of great sex.

You need to feel good where you live – it's the base for your life, the place you set out from and return to, the place where you eat and love and spend your relaxation time, the place perhaps where you work or find inspiration for your work. It's also the home of your sexuality and probably the place where you have sex. So it's important to feel at home there, pleased with your surroundings, and just as at one with the ambience as you are with your inner self and your partner.

First and foremost – situation

When you choose a home, make every effort to find a place where you enjoy the approach as well as the feeling of getting inside the door. Somewhere, whatever the size, you're glad to come home to.

How to set about making your home into a sensual haven

Remember the other secrets and incorporate them in your surroundings:

❤ Think colour – choose the ones that make you sing.

❤ And textures – have fabrics that feel sexy and look great too. Drape silks and satins and velvets if you love their feel, or hessians and cotton weaves and linens if that's you; whatever, as long as it makes you feel wonderful.

❤ And scents – whatever you and your partner love.

❤ And feasts.

❤ And brilliant music.

LIVE AND LOVE IN THE LIGHT

The aspect of your house and especially its windows has a strong influence on your health, sexuality and sex life. You need light to thrive and probably flourish best in light from the south, west or east.

❤ If you like to make love in the morning, make sure your bedroom has an east-facing window to wake you and your passion early.

❤ If you often have sex in the daytime, light from the south is good.

❤ If you're often free to have sex as the sun goes down – a magical time as the beauty fires your sensuality – think west-facing.

* *

MAKE YOUR BED A LOVE NEST

Your bed is the main foundation for rest and sex. When you have the house to yourself it's fun and often erotic to make love in other parts of it, but inevitably you'll find yourselves gravitating back to the bed – it's comfortable and familiar, so it's easy to relax and concentrate on the sensuality you're sharing. Make it attractive to all your senses.

♥ Buy the best bed you can afford; a sturdy base and firm, well-made mattress will pay dividends for your sex life for years.

♥ Add good-quality bedlinen that looks terrific and feels good to the touch too.

♥ Don't skimp on duvets or blankets in any sense – choose top of the range for warmth and lightness and the wonderful way that best-quality quilts and blankets drape softly against your body. It's worth paying a premium – you're worth it and so is your sex life.

♥ Adorn your bed with a generous number of luxury-quality pillows, not just because you'll sleep better with a good support but because they're useful for all sorts of sexual positions.

♥ Add sensuous touches by draping silk scarves, maybe, or buying gorgeous bathwraps to wear.

♥ Make sure the room's warm – you'll want to shed your clothes without goosepimples!

♥ Place the bed with its head against the north or east wall of the room – for deepest relaxation while you sleep, for creative dreams and to replenish your sexual energy.

* *

A FINAL BEDROOM TIP FOR A BRILLIANT SEX LIFE

Keep your bed and your bedroom inviting so that it's always a pleasure returning to it.

♥ Dress the bed attractively; always make the bed when you get up so it is welcoming.

♥ Keep it sexily fragrant to spark desire by placing a tissue sprayed with your or your partner's scent between the pillows or inside the bedclothes.

♥ Have scented candles in the room ready to light when you feel like romantic sex – they'll light and perfume the room seductively.

♥ Have a no arguing, no fighting, no talking about money rule in the bedroom. Keep it a neutral zone of peace and sensuality.

Cherish your home – however simple or luxurious. Make it a safe, warm, comfortable, sensually pleasing place to be. It's all part of loving yourself and so part of the circle of beautiful sex.

The Seventh Secret:
Your Soul – The Catalyst

❤ ❤

Mind-blowing sex feels like magic, but you create it yourself by gathering together the essential elements. Desire, arousal and climax dance with an inspiring and satisfying emotional mix and are joined together by an amazing catalyst – spiritual joy – which fuses them into the completest harmony imaginable.

Many get there when they're in-love: it's as though the combination of physical and emotional attraction lifts you automatically into the spiritual realm, so that you can let go and taste the heaven on earth ingenuously. But you don't have to be in a state of infatuation. Mind-blowing sex can feature throughout your life and carry on fulfilling even the longest-lasting relationship. And you can bring it about.

The final, catalytic secret of mind-blowing sex – the key to encouraging truly fulfilling sex into your life and holding it there as an ongoing fixture – is all-round health in its true sense, the life-force of vitality in mind, body and spirit. Health – a continuous, positive, energy-infused state of healing. For with your body in tune with your emotions and your spiritual essence, you have the foundation for the sexual wholeness you've always known can be yours.

Replenish your natural reserves and re-charge your sexuality

Help yourself to the kind of all-round health where your sexuality can flourish. Everything in this book gears you to maximize your innate potential to shine with energy and lavish love and attention on your senses. In so doing you boost your immune system and help your body and mind replenish their natural resources and reserves. The spin-off is that your sexuality recharges and in turn boosts your overall health – another of the precious circles of interaction that our bodies thrive on.

Three of the most effective sources of inspiration and energy for your general health, happiness and the natural spin-off of joyous sex, are meditation, relaxation and self-healing. They are yours to use and enjoy. If you get into the habit of paying them attention every day they will make a tremendous difference to your life – and your sex life.

Together they form the most powerful secret of mind-blowing sex of all; for they unlock the others, making them easily accessible. And even alone they have the power to transform sensuality and sexuality. Let's look at meditation first.

The Magic of Meditation

Meditation soothes the soul and gives a relaxation to mind and body profounder than the soundest sleep. It's another dimension – like going down a level in a lift in your mind to the core of your being. You don't lose contact with reality and wakefulness as you do in sleep; all the time you are alert and in a sense more alert than at any other time. But you pay no attention to your senses or outer influences for meditation is to be in contact with your inner self and the energy of life itself – focused and absorbed.

There are many levels to the art of meditation. It's easy to learn to meditate purely to relax and calm yourself, and with more practice you can soon become accustomed to listening for and contacting a spiritual dimension.

Meditation, meaning and sex

Meditation is a wonderful way to relax, recharge your batteries and give yourself the chance to be in touch with your inner being. The deep calm and increase in self-knowledge that come with regular practice of meditation together strengthen your self-esteem, help you forge strong relationships and develop your ability to love and care for others.

For your sexuality and sex life, meditation opens a door in your mind allowing you to walk through to a new, uncluttered place of consciousness where you can freely appreciate all your senses and sexual responses with no fear or prejudices. Sex can be seen for the gift of joy it is, untouched by negative experience or attitude.

When you come out of meditation and back into the reality of the mixed emotions and physical impressions of your sexuality and sex life, you are more capable of relating to your partner positively, constructively and lovingly. For meditation, like great sex, is all about love both of self and others.

Sex in perspective

It's also about a deep respect for our environment and the energy or life force behind it. For many it's an expression of their faith in God or the power of the universe. And this too is helpful in integrating sexuality into your life comfortably and fulfillingly, for it enables you to see your own wants, needs, longings and relationships in perspective.

When you meditate your mind is in total harmony with your body; eventually it enables you to develop a deep feeling of self-love, respect and dignity. You can start to feel whole, but also safe in your place within this universe. Also, a surprise bonus is that it can make a tremendous difference to your sex life, since meditation increases your energy levels.

An elixir of life

You feel fantastic when you meditate regularly – it's like drinking an elixir of life. Creativity flourishes too and that also has a brilliant effect on your sex drive. Go on, try it: next time you feel your creativity is blocked or sluggish, take time out – even twenty minutes will do – to meditate. Then take another look at whatever project you've in mind. You'll see it with new eyes, fresh ideas and deeper understanding. And when you're in flow creatively you'll feel together, full of life and deep down sexy. So meditate to recharge as often as you are able.

More power to your meditation – and your relationship

Meditation makes it easier to be yourself, to value yourself and at the same time respect and empathize with your partner. The ongoing power of meditation lights up understanding and empathy.

Meditation and you – learning the way

When you start to practise meditation you need to be alone or with others committed to stillness and quietness as they too meditate. Make sure anyone else in the house knows that you are not to be interrupted and take phones off hooks, or if necessary put the answerphone on for immediate answer with the sound turned right down so you won't be distracted.

Choose a place where you feel comfortable. Many believe the earth's energy or magnetic fields flow longitudinally or latitudinally, so ideally face one of the compass points – north, east, south or west. I'm usually drawn towards a west-facing axis but some religions believe facing east is the best position for spiritual sensitivity. Do what feels relaxed for you. If you're not sure of the direction your home faces, you can use a compass to check your alignment or note which windows face the rising and setting sun.

Your position is important: you need to be comfortable and straight-backed. Any of these are fine:

♥ Cross-legged – you'll need a couple of cushions under your bottom to make this comfortable.

♥ A sitting kneel – sitting back into your ankles with a cushion or two under your bottom for padding and to raise you a little.

♥ Lying flat on your back, legs outstretched and, if you like, with your feet raised and supported by a cushion.

♥ Lying flat on your back, legs bent and drawn up towards you so the front of your thighs are resting against your stomach.

♥ Sitting in a chair, arms and legs uncrossed, feet on the floor.

However you choose to meditate, keep your back straight so that the back of your head is in line with your back. Make sure that your rib cage is lifted, so you're not slouching and can breathe easily and deeply.

It's important to find a position that feels good, but composed and alert. If you feel tense, run through this relaxation technique:

1 Breathe deeply three times – imagining yourself letting go of tension with each out-breath, and taking in calm and confidence with each in-breath.

2 Focus on and relax each part of your body in turn. Start with your eyes – widen them and then let the tension fall away. Then neck – tensing then easing, shoulders, elbows, hands, chest, stomach, hips, thighs, knees, calves, ankles, feet and toes.

3 Then tense all your body, and let go.

4 Now think of yourself as letting go emotionally too. Imagine all your fears and anxieties and negative thoughts dropping away from you.

5 Now be still. A pause. A waiting. Peace.

6 Let everything go. Just be.

You may like to meditate with your eyes closed or prefer to look at the flame of a candle. It can be as simple as that, but especially while practising initially you may need a ritual to settle into meditation and a deep level of relaxation.

Having a specific route into meditation also helps you ignore day-to-day thoughts and worries that stray into your mind.

Chanting a mantra can be effective in stilling the mind and inducing a meditative peace. Choose a word which has good connotations for you and whose sound you like – a word with a positive meaning and flowing sound – for example, harmony, gently, love. Say the word quietly to yourself over and over again as though chanting a hymn. If you try several words and can't find one which helps you still your mind, you might prefer the classic 'Om'. Try it. The way it hums gently at the back of your throat and neck is extremely soothing.

Or try my meditative path:

1 Imagine you are going to walk up a flight of steps. See them in your mind. You know you are going to enjoy the climb.

2 Take the first step and carry on, counting your steps in threes – left right left, right left right, left right left.

3 Concentrate on taking each step and feel it in your mind as though you actually are: how the surface feels under your feet, the effort, depending on the rise between them, to take the next step.

4 After nine steps you may already be in the swing of climbing, and if so you're ready to go on. If not, keep going until the rhythm of taking steps upwards has focused your mind completely.

5 Now imagine yourself stepping on to the grassy path you've reached at the top of the flight of steps.

6 Walk up its gentle incline imagining your favourite flowers or blossom trees growing on either side, their scent drifting over you and mingling with the sweet smell of the grass beneath your feet.

7 After a hundred yards or so the path opens out and you'll see you've come out on to a grass-topped hill with the ocean or a wonderful countryside view opening before you.

8 You see an imaginary friend in whom you've total trust is waiting for you.

9 A sense of warmth, love and welcome suffuses you and you know you are safe.

> **10** You sit and look out at the view and, if you wish, imagine yourself floating into it, drifting in a gentle breeze. You have a deep sense of peace.

Now you can simply be in the peace of meditation if you wish. Stray thoughts will probably keep surfacing. Simply notice them and gently let them go by focusing on the calm of just being in your special place – safe, loved and utterly content.

Or you can choose a different meditation, to enable fresh understanding. So if you have been pondering a decision, or you're worried about someone or something, or if you are seeking a new direction but don't know where, simply ask, in your mind, for understanding and, if needed, guidance. Then wait quietly, listening. Sometimes an answer will come to you, perhaps in a sense of the situation in question being illuminated so that you can see it clearly and know you will now be able to find your own answers. Or it could be as direct as though you are given specific guidance. But the most usual way, I find, is that the meditation continues quietly as a peace-finding, listening time, and the answers come to me later, at any time of the day or night, as though the meditation has cleared my mind and allowed them through.

Whatever the nature of your meditation, it will benefit your sexuality and relationship. By lifting the pressure of fatigue or stress you'll be able to value yourself and your partner more and find a better balance both personally and together.

Healing, replenishing and renewing

Every cell of your body is in a constant process of change, growing and renewing. Your mind, too, is maturing all the time and it's up to you to keep it lively, open to new ideas and learning, questioning and thoughtful. You're a work of art – a work in progress. Keep reviewing yourself, your life, your relationship, your emotions, your sexuality – and keep honing and adjusting and growing. Love life to the full – fresh and positive and shining fit. Keep thinking, always aware of the world around you and your attitude to it. It doesn't matter whether you've a PhD or never passed an exam in your life – it's the quality and energy of your thinking that counts. When your whole life is in positive gear your sex life will be too.

And your sexual magnetism will be strong and sure

Yes, physical health is sexy – and it's attractive to have glossy hair, clear skin, good muscle tone, etc. But it's personality that fires attraction in the long run. The appeal of the most fantastic looks in the world will soon dim if they house a dull personality.

So think vibrantly. Take an interest – in all sorts of different aspects of your life and life generally. This is such an extraordinary world, it's easy just to get overwhelmed with all the masses of options available and end up doing nothing. You don't have to suddenly start being amazingly active. Just open up your mind to possibilities.

▶ *Shaking up an idea*

Take an idea – play with it – let more ideas flood in – take an interest in them – pick and choose or try them all – add a dash of enthusiasm, a sprinkling of energy – and enjoy. Notice how alive you feel when you do something new or inject some extra energy into a favourite pastime. Creativity energizes you. It feels great and it's very, very sensual.

Start right here

Start with one of the ideas in this book maybe – like looking at the impact colour has in your life. Or read a book on the train or listen to a talking tape of one in the car on your way to work. Or think how feng shui is working in your home and your relationship and if necessary do some rearranging. If you're not working take up some studies. Get interested. Be involved. You are the immediate source of power behind your life; you can revolutionize it. Positivity, happiness, love, feel-good sexuality – you hold the keys to all these in your own mind.

Just thinking all this through is healing and even the smallest spark of interest can start a chain reaction that will one day soon surge with energy and power.

Help it along by looking after your body – loving yourself, every inch of yourself and caring about the way you eat, exercise, dress, moisturize your skin. Look at my lists of favourite books to help and order them from the library or spend an hour in a good bookshop every now and then browsing through others in the health and mind/body/spirit sections. Start walking – every day get out there for half an hour at least, rain or shine. As well as toning up your body generally you'll take in precious light, and invigorate your mind just looking around you. Check out, continually, your impressions – that way you'll always be replenishing creativity reserves and giving yourself fodder for ideas.

Interest in yourself, others and the world around you is crucial to the kind of high self-esteem that turns on the lights in your life and it's essential, too, for your attractiveness and sex appeal. You need to feel good to flourish, and if you want to get there you will – in a constant, ongoing replenishment of health.

One of the most healing things of all is love. You've probably noticed that throughout this book I've steered away from the subject of love except in the context of self-love and self-esteem. It's not I don't believe in it – on the contrary I believe it's the most important power there is, and all through this book it's been the underlying mainstay. Everything good comes down to love – consciously or not. But there are many sorts of love and to get into all the complexity would have confused the subject of mind-blowing sex and could easily take up volumes all on its own.

But we need to take a look at its place in health and its impact in healing.

Perhaps, if I just say love is health, that says it all. Yes – you could keep your body healthy without love for yourself or others, and with no one loving you. But your mind? No; it would be a pretty sorry state of affairs if life was truly loveless. And as we've seen right the way through, self-love has a powerful effect on every aspect of your body and most especially your sexuality and sex drive. Some other examples of the power of love in health: there's the way loving nursing has a miraculous effect in quickening the healing process in medical situations. Having a pet to love and be loved by transforms many a once-lonely life to something wonderful again. Love of God or a higher power or the amazing universe, or a positive faith like humanitarianism – all turn on the lights and make life worth living. Love and care of yourself heals too and lets you dance with life. And a loving attitude facilitates positive thinking and, again, transforms your world. And then there's love of others, and the special partner you may share life with – all valuable in their own right.

But most important, in your sexuality and ability to enjoy the best of sex, is self-love. With it you can enjoy the world the way you want. It opens all the doors of healing. It's the foundation for enjoying life and essential in sexual fulfilment.

Whats the difference between meditation and prayer?

You'll probably find that if you talk about meditation, healing or self- and universal-love, you'll be asked to explain the difference between meditation and prayer. Someone once explained it to me this way: meditation is listening, prayer is talking. In both you can ask for – and receive – answers. Perhaps they are both part of the same thing – a way, a marvellous way, of connecting with your inner self, your intuition; a way of communing with the power of good beyond our immediate understanding. But how wonderful that in prayer we can talk to the higher power – a direct, instant line. We have a fundamental need and longing to worship something more than can be contained in us and our world. Something all powerful, all good. A power of pure love. It's all about awe and wonder, gladness and respect, and we can translate it into an earthly respect for each other, an essential dynamic for any good relationship and especially for a sexual one.

Many of life's problems have relationship difficulties at their heart and many of those are caused or linked with sexual issues. Meditation can be extremely therapeutic when seeking to resolve or remedy such difficulties. Sometimes it offers a clearer perspective, sometimes it lets new ideas through. Likewise, something deeper, different, can happen through prayer. Whenever I've asked for help through prayer, it's always come. Maybe not straight away, maybe in a seemingly indirect route, maybe in a new understanding rather than a pat solution. But, like meditation, it always helps the healing. Try it – I don't think you'll be disappointed.

Let's lighten up!

'Angels fly because they take themselves lightly.' And we mortals need to take ourselves lightly to make the lift-off into the joy of sexuality and sensuality.

It's your choice – you make all your decisions, lightening up included. So think fun – holidays, play, laughter. Take time, lots of time to focus on enjoying life, loving sex. Feel the wonder of the shafts of sunlight that often only pierce through the clouds, but sometimes flood into our lives. Bask in the light and love and warmth.

Did you know what's really behind the quality GSOH (good sense of humour) that crops up in so many dating ads? The hidden meaning is said to be 'loves sex'. Think about it – think about everyone you know who has a really spontaneous, warm sense of humour. Not the sarcastic or cruel wit sort – that spells of sexual repression, bitterness or disappointment. But the *joie de vivre* kind where people let go and dissolve into a real belly laugh, delicious chuckle, or fit of giggles. Doesn't it make you feel great just thinking about it? And laughter's as sexy as wild, upbeat dancing in the way it drenches you in feel-good hormones – and that's sublimely sensual. So seek out the things and most of all the people who make you laugh and share your exuberance.

Sex itself thrives when you share a sense of humour. Gentle teasing, a sense of your ridiculousness, the lovingness of laughing together, all fan the flames of passion and let the warmth linger long into the afterglow.

Laughter is sexy, it's love, it's life, it's part of you. A foil for your compassion in the sadness of life, a warmth to light up friendship and love and the joy of life and sex.

Part 4

Go Wild
About Sex

♥ ♥

Your sexuality is the pulse of life

It's wild and free and miraculous. Make friends with its wildness and beauty and join the flow gladly.

Good sex is beauty and mystery and joy. And it is a part of you. Think, feel and joy in your sexuality to the depths and breadth of your soul.

Think sex – in the round

We need to act responsibly and thoughtfully to others as well as ourselves. Nevertheless, respect the power of your sexuality and remember that sex is influencing you just as much as you are controlling it. It's another two-way thing. Another circle.

Do you sometimes feel uneasy or even fearful about sex, or about talking about sex? It's understandable since the power and potency of sex have, over the ages, been seen as dangerous unless bound by rigid codes. But energy and enthusiasm can take over from fear. Let them. Step by step, if great sex and deep sexual fulfilment is what you really want, it will come to you.

Thankfully we're now free to embrace our sexuality without shame. Each of us, of course, has an individual responsibility to use it carefully without causing hurt to others. But it's time to recognise sex as essentially beneficial. It's not an enemy but a friend. A gift to be treasured throughout our lives.

Sex is something you want and were born to enjoy – a driving force and a tantalizing promise of sublime joy. No wonder you want to make the most of it, who wouldn't?

There are so many things that are good about sex. It's fun to think about it, to daydream about the future or remember past encounters and feelings. Some of the sensations and feelings of having sex are ephemeral. But the energy and feel-good high when you're happy in your sexuality lift you and sweep you along, upping the beat of your life.

Sex isn't something to be set aside when you're not in lust or love. Celibate or sexually active, it's a life force waiting to complement your personality. Revel in your sexuality and sensuality and you'll be more creative, more involved, more alive.

How Often Do You Think About Sex?

Like most people, you probably think about sex off and on throughout your waking hours and dream of it sometimes at night too. But your attitude and reaction to your feelings about your sexuality are heavily influenced by your sexual confidence. If it's lacking, or swings from one extreme to another depending on the state of relationships and other factors in your life, fear can get to you and blame or shame will do their utmost to drive your awareness and enjoyment of your sexuality underground.

Don't let it sabotage your sexuality and the ability to enjoy it to the full. It's the gift you've been given to enjoy – it's your right to feel good about your whole self.

So look at what sex means to you, and see from there how you can take advantage and appreciate it to the full. Explore your real feelings and widen your sexual thinking, going for positivity and a real, 100 per cent genuine love of sex and sensuality.

That means not settling for the mediocre, but insisting on best:

▶ *good feelings*

▶ *mindful awareness*

▶ *great technique*

▶ *a positive sense of your present and future sexuality*

▶ *wonderful daydreams and fantasies*

This is your life, this is your story, so write it well. No one else, however rich or beautiful or talented, can give you the most precious thing of all – being comfortable in and with yourself. For that you need to feel at one with your sexuality and your sex life. They are of inestimable value – and yours to give yourself.

Changing your sexual mindset

If you're not very positive about sex you can change if you want to. Like with many things in life, you can't make progress until you've taken a step back, taken stock and rested steady for a while.

Sex is like that. Initially, call a halt. However your sexuality is to be improved, it's imperative you slow down, stop and stand back from it. You need to see where you are.

Help the process of positive change by asking and answering these crucial questions to deepen your self-understanding. Write down your responses as the answers come into your head. Why write? It's easier to be true to yourself – it's there in black and white on the page to keep you answering from your heart and your integrity.

When did you first register sexual feelings?
Re-live them. Where were you, what were the sensations? How did you feel about it? Did you know what was happening, or was it a mysterious surprise? Did you think, I'd love to feel that again, or no, that must be wrong, I'll pretend it didn't happen?

It's surprising how many people think only of their first fully fledged experience of intercourse or heavy petting. But although that will have influenced your mindset on sex, the very first experiences formed the ground in which your sexuality originally anchored.

So spend a while with them. It may take a while to remember exactly when you became aware of sexual sensations.

Did you feel good about your sexual awakening?
Or had you been told it was something you 'shouldn't' feel or take an interest in? If so, give the child you once were a gentle, loving hug in your mind and tell them they were just fine. You are just fine and every sexual part of you is too.

Imagine how, ideally, you would have liked your first sexual awareness to be. If it matches the reality, fine, re-live it now, warm in the feelings of pleasure and gladness. If it was less innocently joyous, or infused with negative feelings, let go of them and replace them with the ideal. Use the chapters on fantasy and meditation and healing to help you.

Give yourself permission to accept your past, present and future sexual sensations with wonder and happiness.

Sex and you in your teenage years
At puberty and during adolescence there are more stages of sexual transformation. You'll have stretched your knowledge, both physically and emotionally.

Perhaps as a teenager you were full of wonder but drew back in alarm much of the time. Or did you go for sex, unrestrained? Think back and explore the territory again. What did those years and their sexual connotations mean to you. What do they mean to you now?

Who did you fancy?

Who did you have a crush on?

Who did you turn down?

What did you feel when you first snogged someone?

What did you feel when you first had a climax with a partner during sex?

How did you feel about each?

What effect did it have on your sexuality and attitude to sex?

How do you feel about it now as you look back?

Get in touch with your feelings again; they are part of you. Leave any negativity in the past and move forward matured by what you've learnt about yourself.

Your relationships

Now it's their turn to go under the spotlight – the relationships with partners you really cared about and wanted, whether or not it happened, to be with and stay with.

List every man or woman who has been important to you sexually. Remember the build up to sex, register the turning points along the way that moved the desire forward. Go back into your mind at that time. How did you feel, what did it mean to you? It's hugely important to make friends with your sexual self and to do that you need to understand your background, for it helped form your current sexual attitude.

The vital information is the approval they fed back to you and the self-approval it fostered. Without 100 per cent positive approval, your sexual ego will have been pushed in, a little or a lot. Maybe there was no relationship, just a crush on your part. It can still hurt like hell; the yearning, the disbelief that the chemistry you were so sure of was an illusion.

Worse, when a partner backs out once a relationship is under way, or after years of commitment. All are an onslaught on your sexual confidence. Sometimes the healing process is incomplete and bitterness, or jealousy, or all manner of other negative feelings remain, focused around your sexuality, barring or imprisoning true, uncluttered fulfilment in subsequent relationships.

If you think this has happened to you, reflect on it. Highlight any details that flash into your mind: sad or moving moments, cutting comments or actions, anything which may have affected your attitude to sex. Imagine yourself healing, and know that you can and will heal.

Now and the future are yours to enjoy your sexuality as you wish but denying the past doesn't work – redressing it, accepting it, does. It helps to forgive any people who inflicted negativity or hurt too. Let them be – they were caught up in their own tangles and confusions. But you are a free, questing spirit. You can build on what came before once you accept it and let it go. So shake off the tendency to keep reacting to or denying old hurts and resurrecting them in your present sexuality and relationships. Move on.

The Way Forward

It's time to revel in your sexuality. From now on no shame, no guilt, no blame, just the freedom to be you and to fulfil the promise of your sexuality. Go back to your inner core – the life within you is a sexual, dancing, wild thing. Think of it, feel it. Think sex deeply and long. Use your power honestly with kindness and love to self and partner. Don't play games or get caught up in circles of deceit. Say no to pretence and faking.

Be your own person – don't be swayed by the crowd
If your friends are positive about sex, confident about their sexuality, and reasonably knowledgeable – fine. You'll grow and mature with them safely enough. But if there's negativity

coming across from them, beware. You don't need their negativity and false impressions in your life and especially not your sex life.

Each individual makes of sex what he or she wishes – good or bad. Like any energy it can be used against others and yourself. Don't ever do that, and don't ever accept anyone doing it to you. Decide right now that sex and your sexuality are going to be only a positive force in your life. If anyone – friend or foe – throws you off course and makes you doubt the wholesome, wonderfulness of sex, get away by yourself and take time to go into your mind and re-think it. Always, always, search for the truth.

That way round, your relationships, unpressured by negative influences, will have the chance to thrive and grow.

Same with pressure from friends and family to have sexual relationships when you're not ready or know it wouldn't be right. Wait until you *are* ready and until you feel good about it.

Ditto with marriage and having children. Never go into either because you know others will be glad, or because you feel you 'should' fulfil a conventional role in society. Getting married isn't the magical event it's made out to be, neither is having a baby. Both can certainly be good if it's what you and your partner want and you're completely committed to each other and the idea. Even then take time to think it through carefully and logistically *and* feel deeply, mind, body and soul that it is right for you to commit yourself to one partner, and/or to have children. Never even think of it until you've found yourself, and fulfilment in your sexuality. Marriage and parenthood would impact irrevocably on your sexuality and sex life – they are tremendous personal statements, so make sure they are passionately, deeply, truly what you want.

Think Sex – in the Context of Your Life

Already your thinking is changing. Sex isn't an issue on a late-night soap or a laugh, sadness or frustration in someone else's fictional or real diary. It's part of the whole concept of *you*. Your emotions, your body, your senses, your thinking, your mind, your spirit, your relationships, your family, your friends. Your self and your environment.

Sex is your very being. Past, present and future.

▶ *You are the artist*

Sex is the best feel-good factor ever. Get your sexuality into perspective. The whole picture. Your sexuality is a work in progress. Enjoy the making – you may have many muses but the artist is you.

A quick exercise to get you writing your own sexual story:

Write down, without stopping to think, 20 unrelated words that come into your mind when you think of best sex. I asked 20 people to do this and they rarely picked the same words. Out of hundreds of possibilities only a few were repeated. Mostly this happened in the first four or five where the bodily attributes cropped up. After that people let go more. To give you an idea, here are their sixth words out as they relaxed into the exercise. Yours may be totally different – just let them flow and then luxuriate in their imagery.

• sunshine • warm hay • energy • hardness • sinking •
• sweetness • colour • intoxicating • me • skin •
• love • warmth • drenching scent • filled • closeness •
• joy • their face • life-giving • high • safety •

Think sex – your way

Be it: Sexuality is elemental, whatever your gender. You can't deny this fundamental part of yourself, it would be to turn away from a part of life and your being within this world.

To truly know yourself, be yourself and fall in love with life and your life; come to terms with your sexuality, love it and be glad for it. Joyous. At one with yourself.

Do it: In relationships, celebrate sex and appreciate its vital energy for it's the oxygen of your rapport. Don't pretend it's not important to either of you. Give it time, enthusiasm, and, even if your relationship is casual, love.

Never have sex mechanically or as a means of control. It is a loving gift to yourself and a thoughtful gift to your partner; of course it can be a great expression of love too. Devalue it and you devalue yourself. Love yourself, value yourself and make sex the best it can be. In an ongoing relationship no excuses – make time regularly – recognize sex as the priority it is. Who knows, there may not be a tomorrow. You are responsible for the day, and for the way you connect with your partner. Reach out to each other and let sex draw you close.

> *Know today's truth:* You are a vibrantly sexual person and that's good. Sex is a wonderful blessing.

Part 5

Take Your Tiger
to the Mountain

♥ ♥

Help your partner find their own true self

The most valuable gift you can give your partner is your acceptance of their character and the way they want to live – acceptance of the person as a unique individual. You don't have to worry you'll do yourself down in any way by paying attention to your partner and being supportive. Kindness and thoughtfulness always come back to you in full measure, one way or another, even if not from them. That doesn't mean sacrificing your own self-esteem. Theirs and yours will, given mutual respect, complement each other perfectly.

We can – men and women – have it all. Freedom of sexual and emotional expression, confidence, and happiness. But your partner needs your help. One of the best things you can do for them is to help them form and express a healthy, open and comfortable mindset on sex. Talk to them openly about your feelings and attitudes about sex and listen to theirs. Compare your reactions and thoughts and grow together.

Even the experts who teach the experts admit they're always learning – our knowledge of sexology is expanding all the time as new research and understanding pushes out the boundaries. No one knows it all – you can always learn more.

You could start by throwing some ideas into the melting pot and letting them simmer while your partner takes them in and thinks. But don't do all the talking, only enough to give them the idea and encourage them. And don't be afraid of silence – it's important to give them space and time to get their thoughts into gear and start expressing them.

Always be aware, in and around having sex, that your sexual attitudes and wishes may be different and you need each other's understanding. Remember that intercourse is only a small part in the wide spectrum of great sex. Think widely and holistically through the seven secrets. Learn together with mutual encouragement and approval.

Make friends with your partner

Men and women have the chance to make friends on a completely equal basis. No more games or unfair divisions of power which could cause deep-lying dissatisfactions. One to one, free unfettered connection is the achievable promise. Women and men are on a learning curve. Help each other find your balance, confidence and joy in the new equilibrium between the sexes.

Women and men long for sex to be more meaningful – neither physical pleasure nor romance is enough on its own. We want to live our sexuality in all its potential fullness and completeness. We want our physical sensations and energy to complement an emotional and spiritual input too.

Your partner's fulfilment is part of your fulfilment, so take your part in enabling it with courage and enthusiasm.

We're all beginning to understand we don't have to pretend, to impress, to try to be all things to all people and especially our partner. All we have to do is to be ourselves and this is not always easy.

So help each other. Give your partner your hope and faith and courage. Even if it's a fleeting encounter give them your all while you're together. Give them your care and thought and confidence in their ability to find the path that's right for them. It will bounce home to you in feel-good factor – good in the doing, good in the after-effect.

Society can't move backwards. We all expect more from life and from ourselves. We long to fulfil our potential, nurture and enjoy our creative abilities, feel at one with our sexuality in all its complexity and wholeness.

Help each other find your own unique balance individually and as a couple. Help each other find direction in your careers and life generally. Listen. Hear. Accept. Help each other practically and emotionally and, just as crucially, sexually.

How one couple relearned the art of mutual support, and revitalized their relationship and their sex life

One couple, Fleur and Matthew, came to me because they were having sex less often and less satisfyingly. Their relationship was growing uncomfortable in all sorts of ways too and they rightly suspected the sex issues were inextricably linked. It took a long time unravelling all the knotted threads which would take a book of their own to describe in detail. But the major breakthrough came when Fleur was brave enough to tap and express the deep wells of anger inside her.

Her resentment had been building for ages because Matthew patronized her. Although the same age as Fleur, Matthew made out privately and in public that he was superior in intelligence, creativity and business acumen. It wasn't malicious – he was just repeating the example his parents had set and because his mother treated his father's put-downs, bizarrely, as a compliment to her femininity, or if they were blatantly rude a joke, he expected Fleur to 'like' his treatment too.

By ignoring her protests he'd damaged her self-esteem more and more, and created a gnawing, growing turbulence in her psyche and their relationship. The discomfort put her off him and off sex with him so much that she admitted to being on the point of deciding she'd gone off sex altogether, or embarking on a string of affairs or taking the 'easiest' (her word) option and finishing with him completely. All this despite the deep love and apparent compatibility which had started their life as a couple.

The solution ...

In theory, which they soaked up, the solution was simple. Matthew agreed to bite back the slights and begin to adjust his patronizing attitude. It wasn't just down to him.

Fleur realized she had played a part in allowing the imbalance between them. She saw she needed to refuse to accept any insult, however benign he contrived to make it appear, and face him with it so he could reflect on what he was doing to her. He'd then use his common sense to recognize the negative impact any patronizing and/or belittling remark or action had on her, and practise swallowing it and instead saying something positive. He knew she was his equal – but needed to put a lot of effort and practice into affirming this.

Fleur led the way, being loving and caring in her attitude to him again, and encouraging him to be the same way with her. She showed her pleasure openly when he valued her with encouragement, praise and a generous acknowledgement of his high esteem of her. He realized that all he was doing was treating the woman he loved the same way he liked her to relate to him.

It took time but both persevered and gradually his new attitude and approach to her became entirely natural. Her self-esteem regained its former healthy balance and their relationship blossomed. Once the knock-on effect of the resentment disappeared, the wish to please themselves and each other sexually not only regained its former strength but hit a new level of intimacy. They'd shared a problem, tackled it together and in the process developed their understanding of their selves and each other and deepened their love.

How you and your partner can tune in to the same sexual wavelength

Every person has a different approach to sex, experiences sensations differently, climaxes uniquely. So empathize with each other's needs and preferences, subtly tuning in to their particular sensitivities and sensibilitiies. Yes, if you're experienced and evidently pleasing, keep going by all means, but be ready to learn more too about their individual ways. Help them be in touch with their fullest capacity for pleasure. There is no one else in the world the same as your partner. So find out who they are – don't stereotype them.

The best turn-on for the most intense, fulfilling satisfaction is a long, slow build-up of multi-sensual arousal. So, even in the most casual of relationships, think through the reality of making it great for your partner as well as yourself. If you don't bother, it isn't only your partner who'll lose out – you will too. Great sex is as much about giving and sharing pleasure as having it. And if you don't respect your partner's self-esteem, yours will plummet too.

▶ *Intimacy is a two-way process so get involved.*
   Think sex – together Practically, physically and
   emotionally you can help your partner find the way
   towards personal and sexual fulfilment; in the process
   you'll move further towards your own.

▶ *Think sex – together.*

The tiger on the mountain

If your partner's not ready or willing to talk and/or you feel you're maturing faster emotionally or spiritually don't waste time feeling frustrated. Leave them be – their time will come.

In T'ai Chi there is a series of movements depicting and focusing the mind on the need, sometimes, to support others by letting them grow, unhurried and unharried.

In your mind you take your tiger – your inner being – to a far away mountain and sit there with it peacefully, content to wait for your partner to make their journey at their own pace.

A spiritual tiger

A man I was counselling, Ray, was confused and disappointed because his partner Pat showed no interest in his spiritual dimension or developing hers. 'She's missing out on so much,' he moaned, 'Why won't she see how fascinating and wonderful it is?' He was even more upset because not only wouldn't she join him in his interest, but she'd thrown herself into her own hobbies so much she'd effectively cut herself off from him. 'Sex seems to have lost its point,' he said. 'We're on as different wavelengths now physically as we are spiritually.'

We looked at the way his efforts to pull her along the same path as him were having the opposite effect of driving her away.

I suggested Ray 'took his tiger to the mountain' by giving up his effort to make her understand his thoughts on spirituality. Instantly beginning to relax as he accepted this was a good idea, he was glad to decide to let himself enjoy having sex with her on the physical and emotional planes again, forgetting about adding the spiritual connection. In time, once Pat realized he'd taken the pressure off, she might feel confident enough to notice the pleasure and fulfilment his spiritual journey was giving him and see how it enriched his life and his love for her too. That way interest may spark naturally in the way spirituality could enhance her life and potentially her sexuality too, along with a wish to follow it up.

Time will tell if Pat becomes interested in a spiritual dimension, but in the meantime Ray is relaxed in his freedom to follow his spiritual awareness and at the same time they are enjoying their love and relationship the way they both understand.

So, when your partner has some maturing or self-development in process it may be best to accept they are seeking direction and will find it in their own way, space and time.

As a sign of understanding and support, take your tiger to the mountain and leave them be. In so doing you will naturally empower them – passive support can encourage and help as effectively as active guidance. One day, they may catch you up and in the meantime you can be content and at peace.

Part 6

The Power
of Two Together

♥ ♥

Sexuality is the inside and outside of a relationship – the inner beating heart and the flow of everyday togetherness.

Without the sexual dimension it would just be a friendship and/or a practical way to share your lives. The sexual connection, however deep and lasting, or shallow and temporary, adds something special and abiding. I bet, however many sexual encounters you've had, you remember each one? That's because your sexuality is vitally important to your body and your mind and vice versa. They need each other. They have a huge impact on each other.

And the impact they make when they're working in tandem, fluently and joyously and in full consciousness of sexuality, affects your whole well-being and enjoyment of life.

In a relationship this impact isn't just doubled, it's astoundingly magnified. The power of the two of you together, when you're prepared to think sex and not just do it, is more profound than most people ever imagine in their wildest dreams.

It isn't a haphazard process though or a matter of luck. You and your partner both influence each aspect of your relationship with your minds, individually and as a double act. Let's take a look: ·

Think compatibility
The similarities that allow you to enjoy being together are the practical foundation of your relationship. Without any there would be no point in trying. But if you're inclined to be with someone, however brief or long the connection, I'm sure that now you know yourself (or are on the way) and are in touch with your sexual wholeness (or learning to be), you won't waste your, or someone else's, time on a · meaningless encounter. Every meeting, every relationship is meaningful if something in or about the two of you connects.

But how do you decide what the relationship is going to be? How compatible do you have to be to see someone again, start a relationship or continue with an existing one? Think about your compatibility every step of the way. It won't destroy the magic, if you're finding magic – an ongoing awareness will only enhance it. But if you see or sense things aren't, in whatever way, right between you, then you can give that your attention. So many relationships teeter on, frequently on the brink of break-up but never quite tipping over the edge. Are you too frightened to take a look at what's going on between you and do something positive about it? If you're in a relationship like this, or have been and fear it happening again, just remember that fear can only keep you imprisoned in negativity if you allow it to.

Go on. Be brave. If you suspect you and your partner (or someone you're considering) are incompatible, face the fear head on. Dithering in the hope that things will get better of their own accord is hopeless. They won't. So take a look at your compatibility or lack of it. Maybe the latter is not as bad as you're fretting or, in the worst scenario of 'Yes it is', maybe you can pull it together and merge the rough edges far easier than you think. Or maybe, if not, seen in perspective you'll realize that some areas of compatibility you can do without.

Make a compatibility picture of your relationship

Tick the things you have in common:

☐ We share a hobby (or several)
☐ We've plenty of similar interests
☐ We share the same religious faith
☐ We come from similar backgrounds
☐ We have similar attitudes to money
☐ We live in the same area or at least viably close by
☐ We like each other's families

Essential in all relationships, even a one-night stand
- [ ] We both fancy each other like mad
- [ ] We have a lot of respect for each other

Also essential in longer-term relationships
- [ ] We laugh a lot together
- [ ] We like each other's friends
- [ ] We like each other

Also essential in permanent relationships
- [ ] We accept and respect each other's spirituality
- [ ] We want the same things from life
- [ ] We have, or are contemplating, the same level of commitment
- [ ] We love each other

Ultra-Casual Sex

Does it matter, for a one-night stand, whether you're very attracted and respect each other? Does it matter, in a serious relationship, whether you have all the other essentials I've listed? Yes, because we're not talking about a worthless body. This is all about the whole you – your miraculous body and your mind and soul. Why bother with an encounter so meaninglessly unimportant that you're not particularly attracted to the potential partner and don't respect them either? Forget it. You'd be risking your integrity with the callousness and you'd risk hurting them too. So make sure you have those two essentials.

You're An Item, Maybe Permanently

Same with the next two levels of relationship. Hold out for the essentials. Some may grow naturally in time, others can be encouraged. But you need them all if the relationship's going to be rewarding. You owe it to yourself so give it some attention.

The 'compatibility' list is another matter. Pick and choose which qualities you'd like to develop or maximize. Enrich your relationships.

⯈ *Sex and Compatibility*

Compatibility with your partner isn't just an essential part of the relationship, however casual or serious – it's a part of your life, your self-respect and therefore enables the wholeness of your sexuality. Better not to have a partner at all than to have a relationship, however brief, that is thought- and love-less.

Think feelings

Don't be scared of losing yourself in your relationship. As long as you are yourself, and never lose sight of what you know is right for you, you can't get lost, no matter how things go. Then you'll automatically stay in tune with your own sexuality too, and never dance to someone else's music if you know in your heart it doesn't suit you. But remember to listen to your feelings: your heart and your mind, your gut instinct and your brain.

Man or woman – we're all scared of entrusting our feelings, especially the innermost ones, to anyone else. You'd think that it would be different with a partner, and it can be. But often, in many relationships, it's easier to talk to friends than it is to the person closest to you. It's because your partner has such power, such influence in your life – you need to be able to trust them to hold your feelings tenderly and not use them against you.

So if you know that you have never or can't always open up to your partner about your thoughts and feelings, or find them reluctant to be open to you, it's time to think how you can start building trust between you.

Bringing the trust issue out into the open ...

How to start talking

♥ Be upfront. Initiate a conversation by saying 'Hey – can we talk about trust because I feel I (or you, or both of us) am missing out on something that could be great.'

♥ Agree a basic ground rule: that you can both express your thoughts on trust without fear of them being mocked or rubbished.

♥ That way you can both throw first thoughts and ideas into the melting pot to act as triggers for more understanding, more ideas.

♥ Throw in – for starters – what trust means to each of you. Here are some ideas – do you go along with them?

TRUST IS:

♥ A safe haven – somewhere you can each let go of your emotional and sexual inhibitions.

♥ The wonderful freedom to express thoughts, feelings and ideas knowing they'll be valued and if possible accepted and appreciated too.

♥ Lots of reassurance that you'll respect each other's feelings and accept them even if you don't always understand completely.

♥ Showing your esteem and care for each other with thoughtfulness and day-to-day kindness.

❦ Knowing you will consciously avoid doing anything that might hurt each other.

❦ Knowing you will renew your commitment to each other in a continuing process or if this is difficult talk about it constructively.

❦ Encouraging each other to stay in touch with feelings and express them.

❆ ❆

Why sharing feelings is such an important part of trust
Sharing thoughts and feelings helps you connect with each other in the first place. It allows you to know your partner, not just skate around the image they show the world, which is probably only part of their full story. And an ongoing update helps you grow and change together through life's stages and phases.

But more than that, letting each other in on your surface reactions and innermost feelings pushes out the boundaries of your togetherness, at the same time enriching your connection and rapport. It's strengthening and gladdening – the best of support.

And it gives an ideal foundation for your mutual attraction to keep renewing and growing. The greatest sex is underpinned with a strong emotional link.

▷ **Sharing your feelings** enables your sexual connection to thrive, sparking and energizing desire and satisfaction. Letting go emotionally deepens the sexual dimension.

Foster pure loving kindness – that's sexy too

As important as honesty and openness are, remember they need to go hand in hand with kindness and sensitivity. Yes you need to be open and let your feelings flow when talking about them, just as you set free your sensations when you're having sex. But however abandoned and free your thought, or your body, you can still keep a watchful inner eye for how your partner is going to feel as a result of your actions. Lose yourself in your feelings and let your partner explore with you. But let your instinct guide you – it will if you give it a touch of awareness – not to hurt wantonly. It applies just as much to the emotional side of your relationship as the physical and sexual.

Abandoning yourself to your sexual and emotional being doesn't mean losing dignity or integrity – yours or your partner's. They will keep their natural balance if you remember you have a responsibility to think of each other as well as yourselves.

Think love

We have such high expectations of love. It's not easy to go into a relationship with a blank canvas for you and your partner to paint your own unique picture. You're bound to be influenced by the attitudes and beliefs of others, and the relentless message from the media impressing on us how covetable 'lurve' is. Hearts, flowers, Valentines, weddings and romance fly at us from every angle. Paradoxically there's also a lot of cynicism: sadly more realistic with many relationships unhappy, one in two marriages destined for divorce and a far greater proportion of living-together relationships breaking up leaving disappointment and hurt in their wake. No wonder some people are decidedly wary.

But both the romantic and cynical viewpoints are distorted, so forget the contrasting hype and concentrate on you and your partner. Don't force love – let it grow naturally. It will if its environment is right and you are both willing and, if not, enjoy the time you have together.

Willing? Is love a matter of will?

Very much so and that goes for ephemeral in-love and the real love that can endure. We choose to love and, every bit as surely, we choose not to love.

The factors in the compatibility spectrum act as magnets, setting in progress the complex sexual chain of action through your body and mind. But at any stage of the way you can clamp down, your mind consciously or unconsciously rejecting the idea of free-fall into lust and later, love. It's up to you to give it the go-ahead.

Does love only come later?

Love can grow out of infatuation or friendship. But it takes time to see whether it will turn into an abiding, rounded love which you both want to stand the test of time. Think of in-love like an annual flowering plant. Its beauty is there for its one season and then fades. Lasting love is a perennial – it lives on, flowering in its turn but, even in dull seasons, holding on to life.

Your love can't put down strong roots until several months at least have gone by, long enough for you to have seen each other's true colours from all sides. Everyone puts their best front forward at first and you see each other through rose-coloured glasses – it's human nature. The reality, once you're both showing and seeing each other clearly, may not be the compatibility you'd assumed.

So don't hurry love or force it into being. Enjoy the mixing time and let the cocktail of chemicals and feelings mature at its own pace.

I'm not knocking romance – being in love is the most delightful alchemy. It's hopelessly, deliciously sexual in the sensualist way. When you're in love all experience is heightened – the hormonal reaction sees to that. As long as you realize it's an extremely potent drug you'll cope with the withdrawal when it diminishes. If you fight its loss, try to hang on to it, rage against its departure the withdrawal symptoms will be painful and longer-lasting.

> **If you're blessed with falling in love**, enjoy the rapture to the full, revelling in all the wonderful feelings. And if it ends don't cling to it. Be glad for the happiness you shared and it will soften the sadness of loss. Then the memories will be a blessing for ever.

But when love is tried and tested, it can certainly endure if you both want it to. It's an ongoing decision, a continuous commitment. Every day you both actively choose to love and live together. I don't subscribe to the grim view that good relationships take 'hard work' to keep them that way. But it's imperative that you're both aware that love needs your attention and input.

Love is your choice. Given that choice you can both nurture it with thought and care: like any living thing your love will thrive if you provide it with the right conditions. Sometimes you'll have problems: with two lively individuals trying to keep on the same track that's inevitable. But with mutual willingness, getting help if necessary, you can keep your lives and love in harmony.

Love is two people linking and sharing their lives but keeping their individual identity, like two circles overlapping:

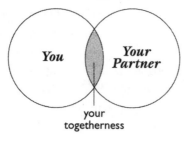

your
togetherness

Sexual attraction is your choice too

Yes, the powerful, lasting attraction that's so much a part of love is also a choice. Great sex lifts a relationship above the realm of friendship and parenthood and practicality. It gives it passionate, vibrant life. It's a foresight of heaven, here on this earth.

A Conclusion – a Beginning
Heaven on Earth – Again

We have always known, deep in our souls, that sex can be astonishingly beautiful. We've known it since the dawn of human civilization. We know it still and the longing to bring the wonder, the essential life-charging joy into its rightful place in our lives has stirred. Perhaps it's a sense of wondrous possibility for a bright new future in this millennium. Perhaps it's because we're at last reaping the benefits of the lessons learned in the last century. But the growing awareness of our potential is surging, and it's time to ride the wave of understanding and harness the excitement and the power.

Use it only for good, never as a weapon. Use it for peace and happiness and pleasure and love.

Your sexuality is a blessing. Treasure it. Honour it. For it is a part of you that is essentially, elementally, mind-blowingly good.

Take charge of your health, your life. Fill your world with love. Love yourself and others, your partner, your God or the universe. Love your sexuality for it is a vital part of you at every age.

Be glad for life.

Be glad to be you.

Make sure the sex you have is great sex - mind/body sex.

And when everything's right for mind-blowing sex, revel in it for it is pure joy.

I wish you pleasure, and a heart of love; a flying, soaring, glorious being in your sensuality, sexuality and the sex of your dreams.

Resources

Further Reading

General information and sexual technique

Tracey Cox, *Hot Sex*, Corgi, 1999

John Gray, *Mars and Venus in the Bedroom*, HarperCollins, 1997

Julia R. Heiman and J. Lopiccolo, *Becoming Orgasmic*, Piatkus, 1988

Anne Hooper, *Sexual Intimacy*, DK Publishing, 1996

Diana Richardson, *The Love Keys*, Element Books, 1999

Andrew Stanway, *A New Guide to Loving*, Ward Lock, 1998

Rachel Swift, *Women's Pleasure*, Pan, 1994

Sexual intimacy, sensuality and massage

Andrew Stanway, *The Art of Sensual Loving*, Carroll and Graf, 1989

— *The Couple's Guide to Loving*, Carroll and Graf, 1998

Andrew Yorke, *The Art of Erotic Massage*, Orion, 1988

Sexual fantasy

Nancy Friday, *My Secret Garden*, Pocket Books, 1998

— *Forbidden Flowers*, Pocket Books, 1993

Christopher Hurford, *Erotic Verse*, Robinson Publishing, 1995

Maxim Jakubowski (ed), *The Mammoth Book of Erotica*, Robinson Publishing, 1994

Lawrence Schimel, *The Mammoth Book of Gay Erotica*, Robinson Publishing, 1997

Relationships

John Gray, *Men are from Mars, Women are from Venus*, Thorsons, 1993

Self-esteem, self-confidence and personal development

John Bradshaw, *Homecoming*, Piatkus, 1991

— *Creating Love*, Piatkus, 1993

Leo Buscaglia, *Born for Love*, Slack Inc., 1992

John Cleese and Robin Skynner, *Life and How to Survive It*, Mandarin, 1994

Krishan Chopra, *Your Life is in Your Hands*, Element Books, 1999

Gill Edwards, *Living Magically*, Piatkus, 1999

Wayne Dyer, *Pulling Your Own Strings*, Arrow, 1993

Shakti Gawain, *Living in the Light*, Bantam, 1993

Louise Hay, *You Can Heal Your Life*, Eden Grove, 1988

Robert Holden, *Happiness Now*, Hodder & Stoughton, 1998

Susan Jeffers, *Feel the Fear and Do It Anyway*, Rider, 1997

Robin Norwood, *Why Me, Why This, Why Now?*, Arrow, 1995

Dorothy Rowe, *Wanting Everything*, HarperCollins, 1992

Vitality

Penny Stanway, *Natural Well Woman*, Element Books, 2000

Aromatherapy

Alan R. Hirsch, *Scentsational Sex*, Element Books, 1998

Julia Lawless, *The Complete Illustrated Guide to Essential Oils*, Element Books, 1995

— *The Complete Illustrated Guide to Aromatherapy*, Element Books, 1997

Suppliers

Aromatherapy Products Ltd.
Newtown Road
Hove BN3 7BA
UK

Grace & Pearl Corporation
6 Lane 97
Tung An Street
Taipei
Taiwan

Natura Trading Ltd.
Box 263
1857 West 4th Avenue
Vancouver BC
Canada V6J 1M4

Neal's Yard
26–34 Ingate Place
Battersea
London SW8 3NS
UK

Index